Having an Impact on Learning

Other Books by the Authors

Parents and Schools Together: Blueprint for Success with Urban Youth

Having an Impact on Learning

The Public Relations Professional and the Principal

Kelly Wachel and Matt Wachel

National School Public Relations Association

ROWMAN & LITTLEFIELD
Lanham • Boulder • New York • London

Published by Rowman & Littlefield
A wholly owned subsidary of The Rowman & Littlefield Publishing Group, Inc.
4501 Forbes Boulevard, Suite 200, Lanham, Maryland 20706
www.rowman.com

Unit A, Whitacre Mews, 26-34 Stannary Street, London SE11 4AB

British Library Cataloguing in Publication Information Available

Library of Congress Cataloging-in-Publication Data Available

Names: Wachel, Kelly, 1979- author. | Wachel, Matt, author.
Title: Having an impact on learning : the public relations professional and the principal / Kelly Wachel and Matt Wachel.
Description: Lanham : Rowman & Littlefield, [2015] | Includes bibliographical references.
Identifiers: LCCN 2015034292| ISBN 9781475820553 (cloth : alk. paper) | ISBN 9781475820560 (pbk. : alk. paper) | ISBN 9781475820577 (electronic)
Subjects: LCSH: School principals--Professional relationships. | Public relations. | School improvement programs.
Classification: LCC LB2831.9 .W34 2015 | DDC 371.2/012--dc23 LC record available at http://lccn.loc.gov/2015034292

Printed in the United States of America

For Maggie, Abe, and Lydia, and for all your peers the world throughout, to whom we wish wonderful lifelong learning experiences.

Contents

Acknowledgments

The authors would like to thank our publisher and editor, Tom Koerner, at Rowman and Littlefield for his continued support and guidance. Tom, your insight is valuable and intelligent. We would also like to thank Jonah Berger for his willingness to pitch in with an interview about education and making an idea catch on. Thank you, Jonah, for contributing.

Rich Bagin, the executive director of the National School Public Relations Association, continues to lead in school public relations. We appreciate your leadership and your thoughts in this book. Thanks to David Luther, a mentor and friend; to Justin Tarte, a clear voice in education; and to Steven Weber, a breath of fresh air—your knowledge is special to us.

To our colleagues in Center School District and in Park Hill School District, thank you for learning with us each day. We feel fortunate to be in the trenches with people like Sharon Nibbelink, Tyler Shannon, Angela Price, Stacy King, Anson Baker, Tamara Sandage, Joe Gunderson, Linda Williams, Melissa Dorris, Troy Butler, Kevin Kozup, Nicole Walker, Michael Weishaar, Beth Heide, Sally Newell, Meagan Patterson, Brad Sweeten, Colleen McLain, David Leone, Kerry Roe, Jay Niceswanger, Nicole Kirby, Shawn Fitzmorris, Jamie Dial, Gina Brooks, Sasha Kalis, Brooke Renton, Rachel Ward, Jeannette Cowherd, Bill Redinger, Jeff Klein, Kristin Havens, Mike Kimbrel, Susan Rizzo, Paul Kelly, Josh Colvin, Chris Daniels, and our Boards of Education.

To our mentors, people like Bob Bartman and Gayden Carruth, along with our professional learning network and Twitter colleagues, thank you for being wise and for providing hope for all of us in education.

We wouldn't get to be the educators and parents we are fortunate enough to be without the love and support from our friends. Justen McKee, Sarah McKee, David and Suzanne Campbell, Joel and Jill Ackerman, Carrie Trotter, Kyle and Kelly Shimmens, Tom and Lesley Creal, the Gnau family, Mike Fischer, and Brett Charles, thank you for being on our team.

Finally, thank you to our families for helping support our careers and dreams. And to our kids, Maggie, Abe, and Lydia, we love you, and we love seeing you grow into the people you are meant to be.

Foreword

Questions for Jonah Berger, author of *Contagious: Why Things Catch On.*

Kelly: In your book *Contagious: Why Things Catch On* and in your professional field of teaching and researching, you think a lot about what makes things popular. This is part of what you do as a professor of marketing, obviously. Your mentor, Chip Heath, talked about "stickiness" and helped hone in your focus on your own topic of why things catch on. Can you help us understand what led to your interest in why things catch on?

Jonah: I had the lucky fortune to go to a junior high school in Takoma Park, Maryland, where I was exposed to math, science, and computer programming—what we now refer to as STEM education. I loved the ideas of statistics, social science, and math and how they all worked together. I liked to think about how the social sciences influenced each other. I used to even tack ads on my wall and think about the science behind them.

I went to a great public high school and had people push me to study social sciences more in-depth. This is where I started thinking about how we could understand how things catch on and how to study it. Now, as a college professor at The Wharton School of the University of Pennsylvania, I teach social influence classes that study companies and organizations.

My K–12 education was extremely important to me. I learned how to take good ideas and started to understand why they spread. And now I get to use all those great ideas I learned in my formal education experience to teach social influence. My current class is Contagious—How Products, Ideas, and Behaviors Catch On.

Kelly: We've been thinking about how *Contagious* fits into education and how it can have an impact on learning. We have some thoughts of our own, but are there ways that you see your ideas working in the [K–12] education field?

Jonah: I like to use the analogy about broccoli. Broccoli is healthy and delicious and makes you better off. Now compare this to a cheeseburger. A cheeseburger sounds better and is delicious but is not healthy for us. When we pick, we almost always choose the cheeseburger. The stuff that's good for us (the broccoli) doesn't win out. It's not random or luck. Some things are tastier than others based on the way people are built.

You can make the same analogy to messaging. Education is good stuff. Education is great work. But often the messaging is like broccoli. It's technically correct but doesn't resonate with the audience because it doesn't take advantage of the science of human behavior. We have to understand what people remember and what makes people share messages, why some ideas are tastier than others, and how to use that knowledge to get our own ideas to catch on.

Kelly: In your book, you write about the STEPPS (social currency, triggers, emotion, public, practical value, and stories) to making things go viral. Each of these STEPPS has a specific value in making things popular. What are your thoughts on how these could be used in education? For example, you write about things going viral because of their practical value or usefulness as "news we can use." You even mention the usefulness of education. We seem to have an inherent usefulness in our product of education. How can we be better at flaunting that?

Jonah: We all share useful information. There are few things more important to parents than their kids. Parents will talk about all kinds of useful information like good babysitters, good television shows for kids, and good food for toddlers. However, people don't share all useful information. The key is how to sharpen the message. We have to think about what makes things extremely useful, so vital to making others' lives better that people just have to share.

One key is to show rather than tell. Too often people think that if they just tell other people why they should do something, others will take action. But showing is much more effective than telling. How can you build a narrative, a Trojan horse story, that carries your message and expresses it in an engaging way?

Kelly: In education, we also tend to have a lot of what you call triggers [easily memorable information that's top of the mind and tip of the tongue]. Triggers are one of your STEPPS to making things go viral. Every day, parents and students are thinking about school and their responsibilities involving school. How can we use those triggers to "market" schools?

Jonah: If I said peanut butter and _____, what word comes to mind? You probably thought of the word "jelly." Peanut butter triggers us to think about jelly. One reminds us of the other. The same is true more generally. How can you use triggers to remind people to think about your idea even when you're not around? What's your peanut butter? Or trigger that makes your message top of mind and tip of tongue?

The key questions are who, when, and what. Who do we want to be triggered to think of our message? When do we want them to be triggered? And what is in the environment around that time that we can link our message to?

Take reusable grocery bags. Most people have them at home, but they forget to take them to the grocery store. And when do they remember?

When they are already at the store, which is too late. People are triggered to think of bags, but that trigger (the store) isn't at the right time. The "when" is off.

The same thing applies to schools' messaging. Who do you want to think about your message, when is the right time for them to think about it, and how can you link your message to something in the environment at that time.

Kelly: Another part of your STEPPS is emotional connection (what makes someone care enough to share an experience with friends). Over thirty million people in the United States have some sort of connection with public schools—whether as a student, parent, or educator. This seems to be a natural fit in helping our topic of *education* catch on—almost all of those 30 million people have an emotion connected to their school experience. It also seems that we should be doing better making the connection of school to the broader audience of our country. What do you think about that?

Jonah: Focus on the feelings not the function. Too often message creators focus on numerical information or reasons, but that won't generate an emotional connection. Think about why people are doing something in the first place. Find that emotional core and you're much more likely to engender behavior change.

Kelly: In our book, we are making the connection between what principals do in schools and how the public relations professionals in those school districts reconcile the two jobs. What job responsibilities are similar? What are different? And how do they fit together to propel the message of education and learning forward? I think your ideas fit nicely into our mission of spreading the message of education. I'm sure you thought your ideas would mesh with corporate products and messages, but did you ever specifically think about schools? What can we take away from your ideas and how they correlate with schools?

Jonah: Word of mouth is good for products, but it's just as important for ideas. How do we build a social movement—how do we bond a community around an idea? By talking and sharing. By being social. There are lots of people who have a vested interest in education—from politicians to unions to parents to teachers. Essentially, everyone is on the same team because at the core, the interest is the same. The interest lies in the best interest of kids and their education. This is an easy bonder because education is inherently something that lots of people have connections to.

The vested interest is there. Building a social movement around education already includes some emotional connection. Use that emotion to build the message.

Kelly: Anything you'd like to add to the conversation about principals and school PR professionals?

Jonah: I wouldn't have gotten to where I am today if not for my educational experience—the system, the people, the help. All along the way people supported my ideas.

Education deserves more attention and more funding. But to achieve that goal, people have to learn about how to build and sharpen effective messages.

Jonah Berger is a professor at the Wharton School at the University of Pennsylvania and is an expert on viral marketing and social influence. His 2013 book *Contagious: Why Things Catch On* is a *New York Times* and *Wall Street Journal* bestseller.

Introduction

When thinking about all the people involved in a school district, there are obviously several roles that contribute to the success of the mission. Each role is dependent on certain expertise at each level—always building upon growth and learning.

As a married couple who share a common work environment, we (the authors of this book) often find ourselves talking about and sharing experiences about school. Sometimes we agree and sometimes we disagree—naturally, right? What we always seem to agree on though is the shared belief that all schools can be successful with the right people, systems, vision, hard work, and tools in place.

As a school public relations professional and as a principal, we have a unique perspective on each other's job. Whether we are agreeing on how the superintendent conveyed her message or disagreeing on how to best tell a story to our communities, we both end up somewhere in the vicinity of *how does this impact students and move a district forward*?

Increasingly, it seems like there has to be a gimmick to make things stick. Like Jonah Berger writes about in his foreword, and why his book is so popular—there has to be a trigger for someone or something to catch on. How do we make our schools and what we are selling (education) sellable? When you combine a school leader and a school public relations director, our conversation is bound to take on a tone of promotion and marketing a product. What can we do to sell our beliefs and make our schools the product of choice?

Underneath it all though, like any great product, you have to start from a place of quality and integrity in what you are producing. Some people can sell any load of bull, but there is no place in education for ingenuity, lack of ethics, or lack of quality when pitching this product. And don't misunderstand, the product isn't necessarily a tangible thing you can hold on to, but it is an idea, a notion, and a truth that what we are creating and producing is a live, ever-changing, exceptional belief in kids and community pushing for a better tomorrow.

The American dream, right? We are in the business of creating the future. We are preparing kids for jobs that don't even exist. Our gimmick is that we don't have to have a gimmick. We have all the components we need to show our world what good education is. But that doesn't mean we still don't have to incorporate various *triggers* to help people remember why what we do is so important. We have to be able to show our communities that education is the rock upon which our society is going to stand.

Principals navigate within schools' everyday thinking about teaching, learning, and taking care of kids—meeting kids' needs. Principals are focused on kids' academic needs, emotional needs, social needs, and physical needs. And at the same time, principals are constantly assessing the needs of their teachers.

A school communications professional navigates within schools every day thinking about how we tell the story of all the good things kids and teachers are creating. The communications professional thinks about the message and how we all sing the same song of student achievement. What does this all mean to our community? Why is this so important?

This book will hopefully help the reader understand how to use situations to see both the public relations point of view and the principal's point of view when faced with certain topics. Intuitively, we know that principals and public relations professionals should always be on the same page, but practically it might be a bit tougher. Does this mean that principals and superintendents or public relations professionals and curriculum directors aren't always thinking about these topics together all the time? Obviously not. It just means that a husband and wife team of a principal and a public relations professional got to write a book together on their respective areas of work within a school system (for the record, not the same school system).

In each chapter you will get a topic followed by perspective from both the public relations director (Kelly) and the principal (Matt). From student achievement to branding to community to social media, this book will show you two sometimes different and sometimes similar perspectives and how they each mesh to effectively put education's best foot forward. Because in the end, we should all care about how our schools look and feel, not only to educators, but to all of our communities. And when we are putting our best foot forward, we are ultimately having a positive impact on learning.

ONE

Public Education and Perception

Items to think about while reading this chapter:
Public relations point of view:

- Meeting new people in education.
- Talking positively about education.
- Talking positively about other educators.
- Choosing words wisely when talking about education.

Principal's point of view:

- Bolstering public perception.
- How the four Cs of education can help create positive perceptions of student learning.
- How project-based learning can also help create positive perceptions of student learning.

THE PUBLIC RELATIONS PROFESSIONAL

When you first meet someone, your opinion is generally formed about that person in the first ten seconds. Think about that. It takes only ten seconds to form an opinion of someone. Scary! So, if someone is forming his opinion about me in the first ten seconds of meeting, how do I make a positive impression in those short seconds?

The answer is making sure that those ten seconds count—in words, in body language, in a handshake, in a smile. We have to think about how we present ourselves to people. This is something we naturally do as we meet new people, greet old friends, and walk into work each day. How we present ourselves to the world around us becomes who we are, but it

1

also has to be something that we constantly think about and work on as we grow into the people we are meant to be.

Also, it takes about only fifteen spoken words (or maybe three sentences) for a person to size you up. Whether it's the dialect, the tone, or the pauses, those words are valuable commodities in earning an opinion of yourself. The way we approach someone is built into a habit. That habit of earning an opinion is also earning a perception.

School districts think about perception as the way that the community (parents, students, staff, community patrons) thinks about its schools. What do people in the direct community and external community think about schools? How do the schools make people feel? And how can forming an opinion in the first ten seconds be important to how schools operate? Remember, there are only ten seconds and about fifteen words before someone is forming an opinion about those schools.

Perception is reality. Unless it really isn't. The challenge is to ensure that a school's perception matches the reality of what it actually does each day. To match the perception to the reality, schools have to talk about what they really do each day. Schools do a multitude of tasks, but overall, each school has to show what it is doing around *learning*.

When schools drown out the noise around trivial tasks and irrelevant stories, the true core of what's important can shine through. Do you spend your time thinking about managing tasks, or do you spend your time thinking about growing others and supporting the vision of quality education (and what that means)? When time is spent in the realm of vision and what a quality education means, the vision tends to become the reality of what leaders want for their schools.

Once the focus on perception and reality really do match internally, the next step is to make sure they match to outside viewers. This is where educators have to continue to do a better job explaining the importance of education. By explaining, it means telling a story of what we do in schools to prepare our students for the future. It's that simple: what do we do in schools that prepares students for their future? This umbrella covers almost everything we do in schools. It's also important to note that the majority of the story about students' futures should revolve around academic performance. Every day is about performing at high levels for schools and students. Shouldn't that be the story told to the audience?

Whatever story we tell ourselves internally and tell others externally has to sync. From the way a person portrays herself when meeting someone new, to the way she portrays her school when working with parents and students, this way of presenting herself to the outside world matters. It matters to that person who is forming the opinion about her and about her school.

Sometimes when educators talk about education, words like *standards*, *annual performance review*, and *state tests* are thrown around in some sentences trying to describe working with kids and teachers. To the person outside the nucleus of schools, this jumble of words might not mean a whole lot, but to those inside schools it should make a lot of sense. We have to learn how to continue to talk about those topics of performance and measuring achievement, but we have to learn how to do it without alienating those to whom we are talking.

This is where it becomes so important to present a clear, concise, and easily understandable picture of what educators and schools do each day. Educators have an inherently good topic to talk about. How easy is it to go out for dinner with family or friends on a Friday night and describe the things going on in school? It's fairly easy. From the spelling bee to the awards program to the progress a student made on her reading, stories easily spill from educators' mouths. When the audience is a known entity, it's easy to relate what happened at school that day.

When the audience is either an unknown entity or maybe a larger entity, it might seem a bit more difficult to describe what happens in schools each day. Again, it becomes important to present a clear and concise picture of what educators do. It matters what words are chosen and what perception is presented. How educators talk about their job, their school, and even other schools shapes the way an audience perceives the product.

For example, when an educator goes to a conference to present on a hot topic, he most likely first talks about where he is from and what he does in that school system. Other educators in the audience are forming an opinion based on those first stated facts. Then, say for example, he mentions that he used to work in another school system and that it was maybe not as good as his current place of employment. What did that educator do? He tried to bolster his employment status by negating the reputation of the previous school district in which he worked. Whether his statement about the performance of his previous school district was accurate or not, he unintentionally diminished the perception of education slightly.

Know this: when educators talk, it matters how they talk about education and their school—not only their own school, but all other schools as well. The better choice for the presenter in the example would have been for him to either not mention his previous place of employment or, if he did mention it, to talk about it in a context that shed some positivity on schools in general.

Schools are suburban, rural, or urban. Schools are homogeneous or diverse. Schools are high poverty or affluent. So many people have a perception about education based on these either/ors. We have to start busting the perception of the *or* in these descriptors. We have to start describing schools with *ands*. Education is for you *and* me; education is for him *and* her; education is for them *and* us. While we will always have some descriptors that carry connotations of certain perceptions, there are ways to help shatter the negative perception that some hold for education.

The first is to be cognizant of what words educators use to talk about education and schools. The second is to have some stock sentences to describe your school or what you do. The third is to tell a good story about your schools and students. And the last is to talk positively about all schools. Remember, educators are creating an impression of themselves and of their school when they talk about education. The opinion formed initially is the perception most likely to stick.

Choose words well, choose stories well, and think about what's important in describing the way schools work. Choose wisely when choosing to talk about your role in education. All those who work in education are spokespeople for the schools in which they work. The sense of professionalism in how we talk about education shapes the way our audience perceives what we do. It's important to make sure public education deserves the pedestal it should stand upon.

The challenge for all educators then becomes this: if we want education to be seen in a positive, professional, honest, and good light, then we have a responsibility to sway our audience with the reality of those things. The impression educators make must contain moral and professional characteristics. The perception of public education depends on the people working in schools. The responsibility belongs to each of us working in schools.

Educators are responsible for choosing wisely when speaking about their jobs. Educators have to understand that what they say carries an impact beyond themselves. It affects their schools and students, parents in their schools, and the community.

People are listening. Let's tell them what we want them to hear—the good news about what's happening in our schools and how important the mission is in educating our kids. Public relations professionals think about this all the time—how do we communicate the good happening in our schools and how do we remain in the realm of vision and mission for our schools.

Tell the audience the things that reflect a perception of achievement and goodness. That means choosing wisely when choosing to talk about education. And it means making the audience form an opinion of educators and schools that is nothing less than professional and positive. Make the impression that educators are teaching and learning at high levels with their students, and do this by thinking about the words chosen to make the impression.

THE PRINCIPAL

If the public relations professional thinks a lot about perception and how an audience feels about a school district, then the principal has a huge role in carrying out the vision at each individual school level because parents and students are going to have a perception immediately upon being connected with a school.

A person's perception is reality. What is the public's perception of public education or even a certain school? Is it positive? Is it negative? Is it neutral? And from where is this perception derived? As a school community, what we do each and every day affects the perception of public education.

Education is the one profession that every person has experienced at one point in his or her life. From the age of five (or earlier), everyone has experienced education at different levels. Perhaps it is a favorite teacher or a challenging subject or a memorable learning experience; every person can relate to an educational experience. This schema in part is what drives the perception of public education.

As society changes around us with the advancement of technology and innovative ideas, does education keep up or fall behind? The perception of education is often focused around the main content areas of reading, writing, and mathematics. These foundational skills are essential and necessary for learners to continually grow and develop. However, education should and must go well beyond the basics. Education must move beyond concepts that can be Googled and move to a higher level of application and synthesis of ideas.

How can schools change the public's perception and model learning that will prepare learners for jobs that have not been created? In comes the importance of the four Cs—critical thinking, collaboration, communication, and creativity (Figure 1.1). When learners can be critical thinkers, collaborate with one another, communicate their ideas and their learning, a high level of creativity will exist. By focusing on the four Cs, we can begin to bolster the perception of school and develop learners who will be prepared for college, career, and life.

Each of these skills in isolation is a valuable skill for learners to possess in school, in a career, and in life. However, when these skills work in conjunction with one another, they allow learners the skill set to be productive contributors to society. Schools are working with each of these four Cs to accentuate and enhance these skills in our learners.

Merriam-Webster defines collaboration as "the ability to work with another person or group in order to achieve or do something." The ability to work with others to achieve something is a necessary skill set in today's workforce and the daily interactions we encounter in life. Working with others to achieve a goal is not always a common skill that all learners possess.

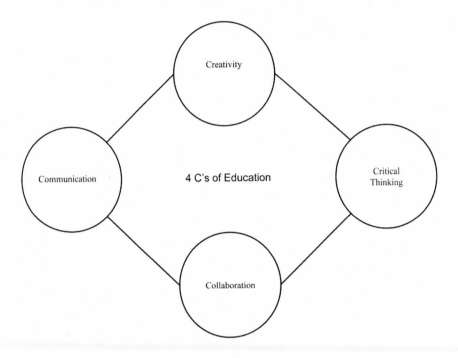

Figure 1.1.   Four Cs of Education

Many different factors are evident when effective collaboration occurs: deciding on a common goal, delegating tasks and job responsibilities, having norms that allow the group to function effectively, agreeing on a timeline, and developing a plan of action and holding one another accountable. These skills should be both explicitly taught and developed in authentic learning environments.

One such way to develop these skills in schools is through the development of project-based learning (PBL) experiences. PBL is a dynamic classroom learning approach in which learners can actively explore relevant, real-world problems, all the while developing a high level of autonomy and mastery of the skills and concepts presented through the core learning experience.

PBL experiences allow learners to demonstrate their ability with collaboration, critical thinking, and communication. PBL experiences differ from traditional projects in many different ways. Table 1.1 highlights some of the key differences.

For a PBL experience to be an effective learning opportunity encompassing critical thinking, collaboration, and communication, four main tenets should exist:

1. Real-world connections

Table 1.1.   PBL Experiences versus Traditional Projects

Traditional projects	Project-based learning experiences
Based on directions provided to the learner	Based on guiding questions and a need to know
Can be done at home or school without teacher guidance or collaboration	Require teacher guidance and true collaboration
Students do not have the opportunity to make many choices throughout the learning	Students make many choices throughout the learning within the working guidelines of the classroom
Are often turned in	Are presented to a larger audience including members outside of the immediate classroom community

2. Collaboration with teacher guidance
3. Student driven
4. Opportunities for embedded assessment

An authentic PBL experience begins with questions around a relevant, timely topic of interest to the learners. The learners drive the experience as they see the connections between school and life and work to create a learning experience designed to answer those guiding questions. Students work collaboratively to answer the guiding question with the guidance of the teacher.

The teacher does not simply turn over the reins to the students and wait until the learning experience is complete. Along the way, natural assessment opportunities arise that let the learners and the teacher determine the effectiveness of the learning related to the guiding question. Finally, the collaborative team presents its findings to the larger classroom community, providing an opportunity to practice public speaking skills.

PBL experiences provide learners the opportunity to ask probing questions and think critically about ways to solve the problem. Learners work collaboratively with other learners and the teacher to answer the questions and are motivated by the high interest and relevancy of the problems at hand. Learners have the choice to decide how the PBL experience will be explored and ultimately shared with the rest of the classroom learners. PBL experiences provide authentic, real-life examples facing students in school, career, and life. They can help shape the perception of how the school community is preparing students for their futures.

In addition to PBL experiences, makerspaces are beginning to take hold in schools. Makerspaces are areas in schools that allow learners' natural curiosities and creative energies to flourish amid the backdrop of standardization. Makerspaces allow for learners to work independently or collaboratively to build, construct, tinker, inspire, develop, and make creations. They allow for a creative think tank to exist where little direction is provided and learners can use their inherent talents and passions to make and create.

Makerspaces look different depending on the level of the students, the funding sources available, and the amount of resources available. Regardless of the resources, makerspaces are designed to allow for creativity, collaboration, and critical thinking. They produce more than consumers; they produce creators who put their dreams into reality.

Makerspaces provide a space for students to wonder and invite them to research some of their wonderings. The spaces incorporate hands-on experiences where the makers often engage in a DIY project. They provide opportunities for celebration of risk taking and accomplishments. And they embrace collaborative interactions from which ideas are generated, shared, and created together.

Makerspaces can include, but are not limited to, technology resources and devices. Some technology resources used in the spaces include a Makey Makey (http://www.makeymakey.com/), a Sphero (http://www.gosphero.com/), coding applications (http://www.code.org and http://www.codeforkids.ca), 3-D printers, and Osmo (https://www.playosmo.com/en/), to name a few.

The perception that education is a system spouting off information for kids to absorb is becoming unlike the reality. Part of what schools are doing around creation and making needs to influence how we talk about the perception. These types of spaces allow educators to focus on the message of collaboration, critical thinking, communication, and creativity. These spaces provide a backdrop to which we can talk about education as an evolving, current, and valuable place where we raise kids to be thinkers and creators.

Makerspaces do not always need to incorporate technology to be successful in meeting their goal of developing creativity, critical thinking, and collaboration. A makerspace can include materials for woodworking, metalworking, textiles (all flexible materials such as cloth, vinyl, leather, and rope and string, including soft circuits and wearable electronics), LEGOs, craft items (pipe cleaners, pom-poms, and cotton balls), and other recyclable materials (paper towel rolls, newspaper, cups, and paper plates).

The possibilities are endless because if one can dream it, one can create it in a makerspace. "Makerspaces allow students to take control of their own learning as they take ownership of projects they have not just designed but defined. At the same time, students often appreciate the hands-on use of emerging technologies and a comfortable acquaintance with the kind of experimentation that leads to a completed project."[1]

PBL experiences and makerspaces allow for schools to develop the four Cs—collaboration, critical thinking, communication, and creativity.

More importantly, they allow the school community to change the perception that learning is focused solely on reading, writing, and math and that everything is assessed for a grade and tied to a standard. PBL experiences and makerspaces provide relevant, passion-driven learning experiences harnessing the motivation of the learners. It allows the school community to formulate the perception that schools develop learners who are prepared for college, a career, and life.

SUMMARY

Perception is reality. When schools can begin to use language that exhibits what we really do to help students learn, schools can begin to broaden the audience's view of education. Moving from simply talking about reading, writing, and math, to showing the important work around collaboration, critical thinking, communication, and creativity is helping shift the mindset of how we think about and communicate our work in schools. Giving students authentic, project-based learning opportunities and giving educators the right frame of mind to go out into the community and share the reality of what's happening in our schools is the way to help shape positive perceptions.

Choose wisely when speaking about public education. The audience is listening and they are waiting for the gravitas that education can provide. The audience is waiting for the good stuff of creativity, collaboration, critical thinking, and communication. Make your message matter. Make your message professional and above the fray. Give the audience the substance they require from an excellent educational experience.

NOTE

1. 7 Things You Should Know about Makerspaces (2013, April 1). Retrieved June 8, 2015, from https://net.educause.edu/ir/library/pdf/eli7095.pdf

TWO

Student Achievement

Items to think about while reading this chapter:
Public relations point of view:

- How do schools talk about student achievement?
- What is the importance of communicating student achievement?
- Academics ultimately prove how good a school district is.

Principal's point of view:

- The primary function of schools is student learning.
- How should principals and schools focus on growth?
- Approach the whole child—social, emotional, and cognitive.

THE PUBLIC RELATIONS PROFESSIONAL

How does a school district talk about student achievement? Is it through the lens of data and annual performance report numbers? Is it through the lens of grades and report cards? Is it through the lens of students and parents? Is it through the lens of teachers and principals? A school district should talk about student achievement through all of these lenses; however, the conversation should always fall back on how each of those components (data, annual performance reports, grades, report cards, students, parents, teachers, principals) relates back to how well students are learning and growing (achieving) at high levels.

The job of a public relations professional in schools is to make the conversation come back to student achievement. Elevate the conversation to reinforce the importance of student achievement. Schools must understand that high student achievement is the measuring stick to which all other aspects of what they do will be compared. Without high achievement, the conversation tends to be about menial topics that schools don't really want to talk about in the larger conversation. Things like behavior, budget, teacher retention, buses, or library late fees can overshadow the mission of what schools need to focus on when people are distracted from the main conversation of student achievement.

The questions should focus on what are your schools doing to support learning; how can a parent support her child at home and at school; what is a curriculum night; what does a parent need to know about student learning; or how can we make our students grow in their learning? When the questions and conversations come from a root of learning and achievement, the other topics tend to take care of themselves.

For example, when a community member walks into the school district office and wants to see data on the school budgets, the numbers tend to be justified when schools are doing well in the area of student achievement. The numbers tend to be harder to justify when schools are not doing well in the area of student achievement.

Also think about student behavior—student behavior tends to be better when students are involved and immersed in real learning opportunities. When the level of student engagement in authentic learning is high, the problems with student behaviors tend to be low. Both of these very different examples of school budgets and student behaviors can be explained through the scope of student achievement. When student achievement is high, the other things can start taking care of themselves.

The conversation can't be about education if there's no achievement. It becomes about other distracting things that dominate precious time and resources. Don't make this an option. Achievement is meaningful when schools make their goals around academics. All schools do this (or should do this)—they make goals around student learning and academics. From that point of reference, the other responsibilities stream naturally.

Public relations is about lots of things, but in the realist sense of what public relations does, it takes a product and helps convey it to a broader audience. Public relations professionals work on the message. What is the message that the broader audience needs to hear? And how is that message shaped by what schools do each day? The message easily becomes about student achievement when all facets of schools are working toward student achievement.

Student achievement can sound a bit stuffy sometimes. Even though it might sound a bit dull, the focus certainly needs to be on the message of student achievement, and it can be done in several ways. In fact, it is good to have a bit of audacity when talking about student achievement because it provides a sense of credibility and lends a sense of stature to the nature of the subject. Doesn't education need to be put on a higher pedestal? Don't we want the air of authority when talking about education? We do. We want the conversation about student achievement to have the sense of utmost importance when talking about education. Have a bit of hubris when talking about student achievement as it relates to education. Have a bit of self-confidence and strength. Warning, though: use *audacity* and *hubris* only when it's warranted—only when the data can support the claim. And if the data are on the upward trend, then be audacious about that claim. Growth is good.

Educators and public relations professionals in schools have to be better about touting the great things students and schools do in the area of student achievement. When a product is good, the public relations tends to be good. And vice versa. When *public relations* is done well, the professional takes the product and makes the audience see it in a whole new way. We can talk about events and student achievement and take photos of students in the library, and we should do all of that. But then to take those components and turn them into a feeling of what our schools produce each day is invaluable.

It needs to be about a higher meaning. Educators work for a calling. Schools are full of feelings of the greater good. The greater good is easy to convey through emotional stories of students and teachers working hard to be ready for the future we know nothing about. That message of the greater good is magical when showing student achievement. Think about making the audience feel a tug on their hearts when talking about student growth and learning. Schools have an inherently good product— kids and teachers. It should be easy to talk about the great kids in our schools.

For example, a reporter asks about the grumblings in your school district about an upcoming election. The way to bring the conversation back to students involves figuring out how to message student growth and learning (student achievement) as the important part of the story. A hypothetical response follows: *The election is something we are certainly thinking about and cognizant of as it impacts some of our school functions, but we're really just continually focusing on what our students are learning and what student achievement means for our students no matter what the result of the election.* Add how important it is that the community continues to support kids in their journey to college and career. That response ensures the message remains focused on student achievement.

How do you make the message of student achievement come to life? How do you show student achievement to your community and to the larger audience of our world? Think about the message as it relates to student learning and achievement. Think about the meaningful *triggers* that will make the audience react positively and emotionally to the message. Think about the *feeling not the function* like Jonah Berger talks about in the foreword. Think about what student achievement feels like.

Student achievement is the only thing that ultimately proves how good a school is. Almost nothing else matters when the achievement is bad. Focus on raising the academic climate and then show the growth through student, teacher, and community stories. The people working in schools should all be focused on this mission of student achievement. And when the focus is on student achievement, the public relations professional can focus on spreading the good news of achievement. The audience is going to be making a judgment based on academics—their perception is going to be based on academic data. Make sure there is some substance in achievement and then go spread the message.

THE PRINCIPAL

Ask this question: "What is the top goal for a child in school?" Answers will vary; perhaps some of the following are on the right track: being lifelong learners, being able to apply knowledge, being problem solvers, having a great understanding of social justice, learning to cooperate and collaborate with others, battling through adversity, setting personal goals, and working to achieve those goals.

The list could go on and on, but very few parents will think about their child being advanced or proficient on the state assessments. Why is this? Are these assessments not important? Of course they are. State assessments are used by school districts and departments of education to track the progress and compare schools to one another.

Student achievement is more than just a test score though. Student achievement is rooted in growth and continual improvement. To help determine levels of growth, it is necessary to have some sort of measurement tool or device to establish the baseline. Excellent educators understand this important aspect and work to develop authentic, relative assessments that provide a level from which students can begin their journey of continual growth and development.

These assessments do not always need be paper-and-pencil assessments. They can, and should, look different according to the type of baseline data that are needed. The data can be collected by administering surveys, which provide perception data. The data can be collected over time by looking at goal completion percentages or by examining and identifying key skill and concept growth patterns. Knowing the type of achievement educators and students are focused on will determine the appropriate measurement tool to use.

When student achievement is discussed, the conversation primarily focuses on academic learning. Why? Student and school test scores are more objective and easier to determine. However, the challenge is to think of the whole child and focus on additional areas as well. Educators should focus on the social, emotional, and cognitive abilities of all the learners. These three areas better define the whole child.

We are doing our students a disservice if we isolate these areas and choose not to look at each learner through the lens of social, emotional, and cognitive areas. Every child is a genius—we as educators have to

highlight and promote these traits and skills for each child to be successful.

SOCIAL ABILITY

All students are capable of being leaders in their classrooms and schools
and outside the school walls in their communities. All students have the
potential to be leaders in some regard. How do educators help develop
these leadership skills?

Oftentimes, when a problem arises, the adults are the ones who manage and attempt to solve the problem. Educators are typically *fixers* and
attempt to solve the problem for others. This mindset does not allow
others, particularly students, the opportunity to share their voice and
work collaboratively to solve the problems. In turn, the adults are having
to work harder than the students, and a key stakeholder is being left out
unintentionally. What are some ways educators can develop student
voice (Figure 2.1)?

- Student leadership teams: giving students the opportunity to provide input in the decision-making process, allowing them to develop their ability to work with others
- Student leadership roles: providing students the opportunity to be
  active members of the school community and develop a sense of
  belonging
- Student surveys: providing students the opportunity to give feedback

Student leadership teams allow students to be an active part of the decision-making process. For example, think about transforming a traditional
computer lab into a more flexible learning space. Have the technology
team remove all of the desktop computers, counters, and traditional
chairs from this space. This allows for an empty room and a blank can-
vas. As the leadership team discusses the vision of what this space would
look like, discuss the arrangement and types of furniture envisioned for
the space. Don't leave out a key stakeholder group—the students.

The leadership team should want to provide opportunities for students to give input and feedback as to what this space will look like, feel
like, and be used for when classes use the space. One way to do this is to
develop an application and send it home with students to gauge interest
in having students be a part of this leadership committee.

Don't be surprised if lots of students return the leadership application.
Applicants might be those the leadership team anticipates, whereas other
applicants might surprise the team. If this opportunity isn't opened up to
all students, some students' voices will not be heard. Make the application brief and think about asking just two important questions:

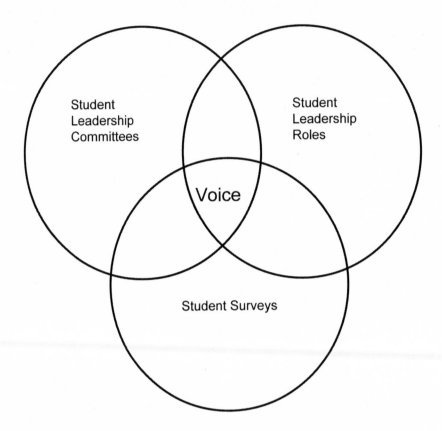

Figure 2.1.   Student Voice

1. Why do you want to be a part of the student leadership committee?
2. How have you demonstrated our school expectations?

In addition, think about asking students to identify one staff member who is able to see the student display effort in his or her daily school work or school activities to serve as a reference.

This student leadership committee can have students that represent every class in every grade. Once the student leadership committee is established, give them a task to work on. Going back to the flexible classroom space example, make this project one that the group tackles.

Bring in various samples of different styles, shapes, and colors of furniture and have the student leadership committee work to identify desirable key attributes. Then translate those attributes into a scoring guide. Have students work with the scoring guide to select the appropriate furniture to be used by all of the students and staff. The flexible classroom, as a result of this process, can be designed by students for student use.

A major tenet in developing social abilities and social learning is creating a sense of belonging. Fostering a sense of pride in school can be accomplished by providing students the opportunity to take on leadership roles within the classroom and school environment. There is a distinction between leadership roles and jobs, though. Jobs and leadership roles are closely related but have a key distinction. Jobs are something you have to do, and leadership roles are something you want to and get to do. Leaders get to serve in a role that helps schools and communities be better.

Take classroom jobs, for example. Did the teacher create these jobs or was it a collaborative effort involving student voice? If the teacher created this list, maybe the list is seen as more of a job list and not a leadership role list. Asking students to identify challenges in the classroom and school and then allowing them to solve these challenges often provides for leadership roles never imagined before. Some examples of leadership roles include door greeter leaders, custodian leaders, classroom leaders, technology leaders, announcement leaders, peer mentor leaders, bus and car rider leaders—the list is endless.

They key is to allow students the opportunity to find their talents while creating a sense of belonging to the larger school community.

Finally, student surveys are an efficient and simple way to gather feedback from students. Student surveys can be used to provide a platform to give constructive feedback from the learner's perspective. The perception data provided to the staff are the reality of the students. Sometimes, the perception is hard to hear, but when viewed as a way to continually improve, the data can be used to better meet the needs of all students. Student surveys can be given monthly, quarterly, or even once a semester or trimester and can be created to meet the needs of individual buildings and classrooms.

The surveys can be developed to provide student voice about what is working from their perspective and what is an area for growth. Even though student surveys can provide meaningful insight through the lenses of students, it is important to remember that this is only one piece of the student voice and educators should remain cognizant of survey fatigue—giving too many surveys, which diminishes the impact and reliability of the surveys.

EMOTIONAL ABILITY

In addition to developing students' social abilities and leadership potential, it is necessary to develop their emotional skills. Schools have changed, and reading, writing, and math are no longer all that is taught in schools. If a student does not know how to multiply two-digit numbers by two-digit numbers, teachers provide resources and interventions. If a student does not know how to summarize key ideas from a text, teachers provide resources and interventions. If a student does not know how to balance chemical equations, teachers provide resources and interventions.

However, if a student does not know how to control his emotions, what do schools do? Some students lack the skill set to handle disappointment, failure, frustration, anger, and anxiety and to regulate their emotions. What are schools doing to provide a high level of support to students who lack these skills?

School counselors and social workers are tremendous resources for school communities. School counselors and social workers can assist in providing high levels of support to students who lack the skills to effectively monitor their emotions. However, not all schools are fortunate enough to have these valuable staff members as a part of their team.

Even if a school does not have counselors or social workers, steps can be taken to help provide interventions to help students develop the skills to monitor their emotional abilities. Developing a check-in/check-out system is one way to help students. Clearly identifying a SMART (specific, measurable, attainable, results oriented, and time bound) goal that will help each student be successful is crucial.

Does this student need to work on calming-down techniques? What about acting appropriately when working independently? Or perhaps this student needs to let others be in charge. Truly knowing the students and their missing skills will help create a SMART goal for each student that can be used during the check-in/check-out system.

One strategy to help students begin to manage their emotions is through a daily check-in and check-out system. The check-in allows students and teachers the opportunity to discuss what the day will look like and provide a pep talk to encourage the students to work toward their goals. The check-out allows teachers and students to reflect on their day. Student goal data can be tracked over time, which allows students to own their learning and take a greater sense of accomplishment in meeting their goal. Before learning can occur in the classroom, time must be spent developing this set of skills so students can better regulate and control their emotional abilities.

COGNITIVE ABILITY

Finally, student achievement must include some measure of a student's cognitive ability. Teachers have a daunting task ahead of them each day. How are they supposed to meet the individual needs of all students? This is no easy task and is not as simple as stating that differentiation occurs in the classroom. To truly meet the needs of students and measure growth in their cognitive ability, educators must develop lessons that meet students at their current levels and gently nudge them to a deeper level of learning.

Many schools use some form of a response to intervention (RtI) model, in which students are given support to help acquire skills and concepts. Often, this RtI model focuses on those students who need remedial or foundational skill help. However, if we are truly working to meet the needs of all students, what systems of support do we have in place where students who already know the skills and concepts also receive support to help them grow and develop as learners?

One way to meet the needs of all students is by examining the structure of the school's RtI model. Can you expand the time of your intervention time or even stagger the times throughout the day? Can you use adults in the building to help provide interventions and levels of support to all students?

By staggering times and utilizing additional staff members (instructional aides, custodians, library media specialists, counselors), more students will have the opportunity to receive personalized learning experiences. Students are divided into groups based on the missing skills, and interventions and extension lessons are planned accordingly. Table 2.1 shows how it might look to stagger times throughout the day in an elementary school.

Having a tiered level of supports, staggered throughout the day, allows for an entire staff to work collaboratively to meet the needs of every student.

Whether social, emotional, or cognitive, students have multiple ways to demonstrate what student achievement looks like. Gear the operations of the school toward always thinking about the impact on student achievement. Give the people connected to your school a reason to be-

Table 2.1.

Kindergarten	9:00–9:50				
1st grade		9:50–10:40			
2nd grade			12:50–1:40		
3rd grade				1:40–2:30	
4th grade					2:30–3:20
5th grade		10:40–11:30			

lieve in the whole child. Show those people ways to use all the talents the students possess.

SUMMARY

When thinking about student achievement, think about how it affects a child. Student achievement can be a feeling as much as it can be a function of schools. There are many ways to help students grow in their learning; it's how we approach it that matters. Talking about student achievement means showing the audience that students learn and grow on many different levels. Kids learn academically and emotionally, and how we translate that to the wider audience needs to be communicated thoughtfully.

Students have a voice. Use their voice sometimes when spreading the message of student achievement. If schools are going to be judged on student achievement (which they should be), then make sure the voice sounds like quality, precision, performance, and success. The only way to do that is to ensure that students are achieving at high levels so that they know what it feels like and looks like, and what it is. When they own it, then we can all go out and show it.

THREE

Teaching and Learning

Items to think about while reading this chapter:
Public relations point of view:

- The importance of having quality staff and quality experiences for our students.
- Developing teachers who understand the message of public education.
- How public relations fits into a teacher's day.
- How our teachers and students approach each day of learning.
- Why this is important to the mission of our schools.

Principal's point of view:

- Principals provide authentic learning experiences for teachers to grow and develop their craft.
- These learning experiences focus on relationships, student engagement, risk taking, critical thinking, creativity, and innovation.
- Principals need to effectively model these learning experiences for their teachers so that the teachers can in turn incorporate these practices in their classrooms.
- All this is done under the umbrella of continual improvement— each day working to meet the needs of diverse teachers and student learners.

THE PUBLIC RELATIONS PROFESSIONAL

When schools develop the message around student achievement, there are going to be all different kinds of people who have a stake in how that message sounds. There are the teachers and principals who have direct

access to students and parents each day at school. There are other administrators (like the public relations professional) who have more overarching access to students and parents. There are the students and parents
themselves who have a vested interest in the message. And then there is
the community that has a stake in the message of student achievement. It
even goes as far as those in the larger context of public education who
have some skin in the game when forming the message of student
achievement.

Because there are so many people vying to have input into what
schools are saying and doing, it becomes even more important to train all
of these constituents on the same message. Public relations professionals
compete for audience attention every day. Why is the message from
school more important than any other message that audiences receive?
Schools have to make the message more important through substance.

What's substantial about the message of public education? The thirty
million people who have a connection to education in this country. That's
substantial. It's important because there are so many teachers out there
who have the ability to spread the message with us. When teachers and
the staff working in schools internalize the message of student achievement, then they have a better understanding of how to say it to their
direct audiences. Start within your schools—this is where the principal is
essential to creating the climate of student achievement because she is
going to set the tone for what her teachers say to the community. Start
within your schools, and help teachers continue to understand their mission of the message.

When there is an army of teachers talking about a topic, it's sure to
catch on. Then not only does a teacher's mission remain teaching and
learning at high levels, it also becomes one of perpetuating the message
of how well our schools raise kids academically and emotionally. A
teacher's story becomes a story of helping that one student be a better
reader and a better kid. In education, good teachers know how to do
both—raise kids up academically and emotionally. Their teaching becomes their mission in life. Teachers are notorious for this—basing their
career on their mission in life. Isn't it why all of us want to be connected
to education? To be closer to our mission in life—helping others and
serving others—especially kids?

As teachers and those working in schools internalize the message of
student achievement, the ease of talking about the topic begins to naturally take shape. So now teachers are beginning to talk about student
achievement in the same terms as the principal, and then they begin
talking about student achievement to the students in the same terms, and
then they start talking to the parents in the same terms. The message is
beginning to take shape through teacher conversations, and then it
spreads to those they interact with. This is how a single school begins the

conversation. This is then how school districts all begin to share the same thoughts.

After teachers, principals, central office administrators, and schools are able to know the message of student achievement and talk about its importance, isn't it easier to actually teach and learn in the spirit of that student achievement? Teaching and learning is certainly about the mechanics of curriculum and professional growth and standards, but it's also about discovering how it fits in with the larger message and mission of education.

Teaching and learning is part of a bigger picture. Helping teachers understand the bigger picture allows them to see how they fit into a system of many schools striving to provide high-quality academics. Then teachers not only get to teach; they get to be better within the sphere of spokespeople for public education.

As public relations professionals, it's important that the context through which we navigate contains a sense of having our teachers be part of our team of message deliverers. What schools say matters. The context matters. And it matters who's saying it. At the beginning of the school year, does the public relations professional visit all the schools in her district and host a mini professional development session on public relations? A short session on what public relations looks like in her school district goes a long way in building relationships with teachers and principals. It could even be an avenue to distribute talking points for the year. Or maybe host some media training. Or highlight some new parent communication tools. Or maybe just have a conversation about students and what they are excited about for the year. These sessions tend to be cathartic, and they develop their own messages about what's important regarding student achievement.

But make no mistake, these professional development sessions send the message that public relations is important—how teachers communicate the message is important. From the teacher level to the superintendent level, how the message gets communicated is important. To have it embedded in teaching and learning is high-level stuff.

When we think about professional development for people working in schools—professional development that revolves around teaching and learning—think about the bigger picture of how an activity contributes to learning more about the art of teaching. If educators think about professional development in that way, then there are lots of ways to actually participate in it. Because public relations professionals' thoughts swim around public perception, we like to think that professional development is one way in which we choose how we want to be perceived. This means that what the professional development educators participate in reflects who they are. How do educators participate in learning? What do they choose to learn more about?

Educators need to focus on this aspect of choosing to learn at high levels with the intent to grow in not only their craft but also in the perception of themselves. This affects teaching and learning because it ultimately benefits the kids that educators are interacting with each day. Teaching and learning becomes an ebb and flow, each dependent on the other. When teachers are teaching at high levels, they are learning at high levels.

This high-level teaching and learning contributes to schools that create successful students—all leading to successful schools that become easy to put in the public arena for discussion. When public relations professionals are touting successful schools, they are really confirming the solid teaching and learning that occurs in their schools. Again, it all comes back to being able to communicate why student achievement (the result of quality teaching and learning) is the most important factor for student (and school) success.

When the story of teaching and learning is easy to communicate because it's working, the audience can more seamlessly understand and see what quality instruction looks and feels like. The story becomes easy to share. It becomes easy to show. Walking into a classroom with a quality teacher feels good. That feeling is understood by almost anyone walking into the room. To be able to then translate that experience to an audience is what the public relations professional can help with. That story affects how a community feels about its schools—all because a quality teacher created a classroom that exhibits high levels of teaching and learning.

THE PRINCIPAL

In today's schools, the learning should not be done solely by the students. The teachers and staff members should be just as active in the learning process. To provide learning opportunities for staff members, principals should effectively model these learning experiences so teachers can in turn incorporate these practices in their classrooms. This constant modeling and learning falls under the umbrella of continual improvement. The principal is working to meet the diverse needs of adult learners who are, in turn, all working extremely hard to meet the needs of diverse student learners.

An effective building principal should model authentic learning experiences for adult learners to grow and develop their skill. These learning experiences can be through informal interaction, grade-level or department meetings, or staff meetings, or through flipped learning experiences. By effectively modeling these learning experiences, teachers are able to experience the learning firsthand and then replicate similar experiences for their students.

Knowing that each staff member is different, has different needs and levels of schema, where does a principal begin? Taking the time to ask questions about sound instructional pedagogy, observing in classrooms, and engaging in vertical discussions across grade levels and teams will provide principals a place to start. Ultimately, an understanding that teachers learn at different paces and have different experiences and levels of comfort—just like students—is essential to providing authentic learning experiences for all.

Ask a group of teachers: what skills do students need to know to be prepared for college, career, and life? If consensus can occur as to this skill set for our student learners, then this is a beginning point for adult learners as well. To make sure our students are adequately prepared for college, career, and life with a defined skill set, it is imperative the adults have a solid understanding of these skills and concepts to be able to facilitate the learning and application in and out of the classroom. The principal must focus her time and energy on providing authentic learning experiences for the teachers. These learning experiences focus on relationships, cognitive engagement, risk taking, critical thinking, creativity, and innovation.

Relationships are the key to developing a comprehensive learning environment. Knowing your people is essential. Take the time to talk with students; get to know them on a personal level, learn about their passions, backgrounds, interests, and challenges. Meet with each student individually. Share about yourself and find connections. If you have not found a connection, you have not tried hard enough. If students know a teacher or principal truly cares about them as individuals, more often than not they will be willing to go that extra mile.

Another aspect of relationships that is critical in learning occurs when a support system is developed. A typical school year has its ups and downs, peaks and valleys, high points and low points. When people know a personal relationship built on trust and care exists, a support system can enhance the learning environment during those challenging times.

A good principal works tirelessly to develop the relationships in his school. A good principal that this author knows sends a picture and a personal note to the parents of all his teachers and staff members. This letter details the hard work and energy the teachers have put into the school year. He sends these notes to let the parents of his teachers know how special that teacher is and how grateful he is for all the teachers in his school. Now that's building a school based on care and attention to teaching and learning together.

There's not a lot worse at school than sitting through a session where a select few do all the talking and the engagement level is at an all-time low. Teachers and students are no different in this regard. On the other hand, when one is passionate and highly engaged, the session is transformed and the productivity level is high. So how can this be modeled to learners?

Asking the students to identify a topic of interest is one strategy to cognitively engage them. Even with the demand of multiple standards and detailed curriculum, effective teachers can infuse different topics of interest into lessons or meetings. Creating hooks to engage students is another effective strategy, drawing upon interest levels of learners. These hooks can be dramatic, funny, memorable, relevant, using kinesthetics, using props, or drawing upon the arts. The key is to find ways to connect with the learners and draw them into the learning experience.

Flipping the lesson, or even a meeting, is another way to demonstrate how to effectively and efficiently use time wisely. If learners can read or watch information prior to coming to the meeting, the time can be spent during the meeting talking, discussing, and learning from and with one another. For a meeting or lesson to be effective, the people doing the most work and the most talking are often the ones doing the most learning. Flipping a lesson allows for more staff members to participate and be engaged.

Also, a culture of risk taking firmly established in the learning environment benefits all learners. What steps are being taken to create this culture of risk taking? Are we creating environments where risk taking is encouraged? Risk taking needs to be modeled, encouraged, and celebrated. Time should be spent celebrating the process and effort, not merely the results.

Young children are much more comfortable with taking risks. As they get older, many lose their ability or desire to be a risk taker. How are schools creating environments where risk taking is not encouraged? Is it fear of failure or making mistakes? Is it fear of embarrassment? Too often the barrier is mental—let's move beyond our comfort zone and take that risk.

A high level of trust must exist for learners to be comfortable moving outside their comfort zone and taking a leap of faith. Trust that mistakes happen and they are viewed as learning opportunities. Trust that no consequences will happen when we have intelligent risk taking. Trust that risk taking is uncomfortable and often met with some anxiety. Trust that risk taking is essential for learning to continue to progress and transform over time.

If learners see intelligent risk taking occur all around them, then they will be more likely to join the movement. Sometimes the risk is organic and natural. Other times the risk needs a gentle nudge to get the process started. Regardless of how it begins, celebrating the journey, the process, and effort will only serve to allow more risks.

Learners should possess the ability to be critical thinkers; they should be curators of knowledge and not just consumers of knowledge. There is a place and a time for knowing facts and information. However, if a learner can Google it and not apply the knowledge, very little critical thinking is occurring.

The questions posed to learners dictate the level of learning and critical thinking occurring in the learning environment. When learners are asked to apply and synthesize the concepts or skills, a much higher level of critical thinking can occur. There are some strategies that are effective in allowing the learners to apply and synthesize their learning: think time, adding on, and restating.

How often do you ask a question of someone and then provide the answer if the answer is not given quickly? Is it because the silence is awkward and uncomfortable? Do we often rescue someone because we don't want him to feel ashamed for not knowing the answer? Providing think time allows for learners to process the information internally prior to sharing their responses. It can be a bit uncomfortable at first. When a question is posed and the learner does not respond immediately, what is only a few seconds seems like minutes for the learner and everyone involved. However, some learners need that additional time to apply and synthesize the information.

Creating an environment where think time is expected and valued is important in the learning process. Simply stating *I can tell that [Student] is thinking and has some great thoughts in his head—thank you for letting [Student] think* is one way to develop the value of think time among the students.

In addition to waiting after a question is posed, it's just as important to provide time after a response has been given. Oftentimes the learner is sharing a new thought or interpretation and the natural response is to praise his thinking. However, when doing this, other learners are attempting to process what was being said all the while hearing the learner being praised. By just pausing a few moments and saying *I was just processing what you just said* can again create an environment where the learners continue to learn with each other.

Along with think time, another effective strategy to allow learners to be critical thinkers is to ask them to add on to what was just said. Using this strategy forces the learners to actively listen to one another and then expand on the prior statement. This form of adding on can take place by having the learners agree or disagree and then conclude by stating why they agree or disagree. Just as with think time, adding on creates an environment where the learners continue to learn from and with one another.

A third strategy for creating critical thinkers is to have learners restate the concept in their own words. By restating a concept in a different way, it allows the other learners to view the concept through a different lens and can possibly provide a new level of clarity and understanding. Restating concepts in one's own words also creates an environment wherein the learners continue to learn from and with one another.

The goal of developing critical thinking skills within students is to allow them to apply the learning and demonstrate their understanding.

Think time, adding on, and restating are three strategies that allow learners to be critical thinkers and curators of knowledge, and not simply consumers.

What comes to mind when thinking about companies like Google, Facebook, Disney, Garmin, Amazon, Netflix, or Starbucks? All of these companies are known for their innovation and creative spirit. Schools should be preparing students to enter the workforce ready to be a part of innovative and creative environments. How can schools prepare students for these kinds of environments?

Look at the physical design of classrooms. Do students sit in desks in nice neat rows or groups? Do local fast-food restaurants have more comfortable and innovative seating arrangements than our classes? How can we transform our learning spaces to inspire creativity and innovation? Being comfortable in changing the learning environment is the first step in creating creative and innovative learning environments. Some of the most creative and innovative learning environments incorporate student choice, student voice, and student design.

These learning spaces could have tables at different heights. Some require students to stand, some require students to kneel, and some require students to sit. Some tables have exercise balls to help students maintain their focus.

The key to making these tables work is that students have a choice as to where they learn. These learning spaces do not have walls covered in premade posters bought at the local teacher supply store. These learning environments have walls covered with student work and student-created anchor charts. Student voice, design, and choice are prevalent in these learning spaces. These learning spaces are warm, inviting, and student centered.

Another method in which learners can develop creativity and innovation is by having a makerspace like the ones mentioned in the first chapter. These spaces allow students to create, make, and design based on the materials present. Technology can be an element, but it certainly does not have to be present for a makerspace to exist. When learners have the opportunity to be designers, builders, creators, and makers, the *in the box* thinking disappears, and learners experience a different skill set that focuses on their innate ability to be creative and innovative.

Teaching and learning must be present in schools for everyone who walks through the doors. Learning should not be confined strictly to the students. The adult learners and student learners should be a part of learning experiences that focus on relationships, cognitive engagement, risk taking, critical thinking, creativity, and innovation. If these elements exist in schools, the curriculum and learning standards will take care of themselves.

SUMMARY

Teaching and learning is the result of lots of educators working together to continually push for higher growth in their students and themselves. Quality educators are the people who influence student achievement. Quality educators propel students to learn at higher levels.

When teachers understand that their job not only influences students but also the way the public perceives their school, they begin to understand the larger picture of why everyone's responsibility is integral to the whole. Helping teachers be better teachers and students become better students helps schools become better schools. This is accomplished through professional development at a district and school level.

It all comes back to being able to communicate why student achievement (the result of quality teaching and learning) is the most important factor for student (and school) success. And when you can communicate that student achievement happens in your schools, you can show what kids (and teachers) are made of. That is what the public wants to see.

Achievement can look like many things, but fostering a space and culture where the whole school is made of learners and creators enhances the environment of growing and learning. Learning is many things: critical thinking, creating, listening, responding, producing. Using all these factors with teachers and students helps everyone understand the goal of learning together, pushing each other toward continued growth.

FOUR

Communication

Items to think about while reading this chapter:
Public relations point of view:

- How do schools talk to students, parents, staff, and the community?
- Taking the school's communication and elevating the conversation to levels that deal with public education and the importance of public education.
- This domino effect of continued communication begins to be embedded in the audience's mind.
- All communication should come back to student achievement and growth.

Principal's point of view:

- How to provide transparent communication with students, families, and the community.
- Use surveys to ask what key needs are and then be transparent with the results.
- There are a variety of ways to communicate with students, families, and the community (website, mobile apps, e-mail, social media).

THE PUBLIC RELATIONS PROFESSIONAL

Communication is a broad word covering many angles of what it means to spread a message to another person. Communication is the way people understand each other. Schools are no different than other organizations when it comes to the importance of communication, but schools do have a greater responsibility to ensure that their communication is geared to

31

finding common ground and bridges to people in the community (students, parents, educators, and patrons). Communication is the way that a school's message is going to make it to the audience.

If schools aren't out there communicating to their captive audience, someone else will be. Schools have to be the ones telling their own stories. Take for example a situation where an outside entity is trying to force an opinion or a piece of legislation or a mandate directed at public schools. This force will be trying to overshadow and remake the reality of what happens in schools. The job of communicators in school districts is to already have a solid message and excellent academic programs in place so that there is evidence to support why schools are already working. Then that message, along with the academic data, supports and upholds the claims of success in schools.

So even before an onslaught of outside forces try to swoop in and influence policies that already have steady track records, communicators have to have already established solid messages and opinions within their schools. Then it becomes easier to combat entities taking swings at public schools.

But communication isn't always about combating messages against the mission of public schools. In fact, communication should be an avalanche of all the good stuff happening in schools—told in the style and spirit of what the overriding message is. If the overriding message is student achievement, then the communication coming from schools needs to be able to relate back to student academic success.

The original intent of school communications departments was to help people understand what schools do—to help communicate the work schools do and to help bolster support for schools. Over time, the communications department has become so much more: media relations, event planning, writing, producing news, relationship building, managing messages, organizing support, social media, website management, content management, community relations, business partner liaison, team leader. All of these skills are embedded in what it means to communicate a message to an audience or audiences.

When educators communicate, it again comes back to ensuring that what they are saying is promotion of the positives relating to learning and growing. All communication ties into student achievement. Whether a newsletter, a website story, a social media post, or a press release, the content of each of those communication pieces should have some tie to student achievement.

Did the board of education win an award? Well, how did that affect student achievement? Form a message like *The board of education is honored to receive this award because it reinforces the hard work we all do in our community to make sure our students are learning at high levels.*

Did a student just score perfectly on the ACT or SAT college entrance exam? That one should be easy: *Our school is so proud of [insert student name] and her score of 36 on the ACT. What a testament to her hard work and the solid academic programs we have in place that have helped prepare her for her college career.*

Did a group of elementary students create a project for a contest that puts their winning work into a local science museum? *Look at our innovative students and their determination to create a project that uses both their imagination and knowledge of biology to produce real-world work.*

Did your maintenance crews stay up all night plowing snow from all the school parking lots so that school could be in session after a snowy day? *Thank you to our outstanding maintenance crew that worked all night to ensure that our students and staff could make it to school safely today. Their team spirit is a tribute to the people we have working for our community and our schools to help students succeed on their path to graduation.*

Did a teacher win the state Teacher of the Year award? Again, easy. *Congratulations to [insert name] as the recipient of the state Teacher of the Year award. This recognition solidifies our confidence in the exceptional teaching staff we have working to help make our students college and career ready.*

Whether these blurbs were part of a website story, a Facebook post, a tweet, a photo caption, a newsletter, or a press release, the content all points to some aspect of student achievement. Even the communication about the maintenance department related back to how that crew supports student learning. This matters because it teaches communicators to always be thinking about how everything we do in schools contributes to helping students succeed. It matters because it affects how the audience perceives what is being communicated.

These instances all involve some component of written communication because the words were attached to a hypothetical website blurb, Facebook post, tweet, photo caption, newsletter, or press release. But what if a communicator needed to respond to a question on camera for a news story on the local evening news? What if a communicator is talking to a group of business partners during a chamber of commerce luncheon? What if a communicator is helping a parent on the phone understand why we have certain requirements for graduation? The *what ifs* can all still be turned into a chance to add in a phrase about student success. We still speak the words that relate back to helping students achieve.

Pick three main points that, as a communicator, you can use to apply to almost any situation in which you are responding to a question or making a statement about education in your schools. Pick the three main phrases that can be restated over and over until they become ingrained in your brain. Make the statements have the flavor of your personality, but also the meat of the message. For example, here are three sentences that can be used repeatedly to reinforce a message of achievement: 1. *What we do in schools exemplifies the spirit of believing that all students can learn at high levels. 2. Student achievement in our schools is the result of collaborative teams of teachers, students, administrators, and parents working together. 3. In our schools, everyone achieves.*

Then drill down to include three more phrases that point to soft data to back up those claims. *Soft data* refers to data that aren't boring for the audience to hear. For example, *our school district scored in the top 5 percent of all districts in our state* sounds better than *our school district scored a 97.8 percent on our annual performance review.* The statement reflects a comparison that might be more easily understood by some in the audience. While it's certainly important that the school district scored a 97.8 percent, the top 5 percent provides a bit more context to the statement.

It's also important to note that while a communicator might be making comparisons, it's not okay to make comparisons to degrade another school system. Like in previous chapters, to raise the stature of public education in our country, we have to avoid the urge to cast negative connotations on other school districts.

Now, back to the phrases that reinforce the three broad statements to have in your back pocket to pull out whenever talking or writing about your schools. These soft data claims need to support the original three main points, for example, *1. Our school district scored in the top 5 percent of all school districts in the state. 2. The technology that our students use for their project work compares to what the professionals at Google use. 3. Our students say that this is a place they want to be because we have high attendance rates and attendance is the number one factor contributing to student success.*

These data claims can be a number of examples, but pick data that are proven and relatable to the overarching message of student achievement. These points of communication can be delivered verbally or written. Memorize them and use them.

Most educators who communicate with an audience (that's everyone) can talk about what they do in schools, but sharpening those words and reining them in can go a long way in polishing the message we want to convey.

The point is that communication takes many forms, but whatever form it takes, it needs to focus on the message. With so many competing messages from all kinds of sources, school communication has to slice through the noise and make the words count. No longer do school communicators have the luxury of assumed credibility. Credibility and trust have to be earned and continually worked on. Communication is the bridge to credibility. It is the way the audience is going to understand the message.

Communication handled in this way then leads to the credibility to be an authority on education in the community, the broader area, and the state or country. This skill to elevate the conversation to hover in the realm of *what's good for public education* makes all schools better. The ability to make the context of education always have tones of high productivity and high achievement raises the level of all schools. The association becomes education equals achievement and success. This takes everyone being on the same message. And it takes all of us continually beating the same drum together.

THE PRINCIPAL

Much of what occurs within the walls of a classroom and a school building unfortunately does not make it out to those who are not privileged to witness the learning each day. Many dinner table conversations are similar to this one:

> Parent: What did you learn in school today?
> Child: Math and reading.
> Parent: What did you do in school today?
> Child: Jump rope in PE.
> Parent: What was the best part of your school day?
> Child: Recess.

Parents need a window into their child's classroom. Schools should be providing that glimpse into the classroom, providing a level of transparency and communicating important information, upcoming dates, and newsworthy learning experiences.

There are a variety of ways to communicate with students, families, and the community (website, mobile apps, blogs, e-mail, social media tools, and face-to-face meetings). This communication can be presented in two different forms: one-way and two-way communication. This chapter will discuss the importance of providing both one-way and two-way communication using a variety of tools and methods.

Merriam-Webster defines communication as "a process by which information is exchanged between individuals through a common system of symbols, signs, or behavior; *also*: exchange of information." One-way communication shares information from one party to another but does not solicit or encourage feedback. It is simply a way to communicate information from one party to another. The most common form of one-way communication is through the traditional newsletter schools send out to their families.

Schools routinely send out newsletters, either a hard copy or an electronic copy, as a way to keep families up to date with upcoming events and important information. These newsletters are routinely informative; however, they do not encourage dialogue or feedback. It is merely a way for the school to share information on a weekly or monthly basis with families.

Newsletters help to provide relevant examples of artifacts, information, and school events in an attempt to provide a window into the daily occurrences happening within the building. Figure 4.1 is an example of the types of information commonly included in school newsletters.

Another form of one-way communication schools often use to share information with families is through the school website. The school website is a centralized location for calendar events, important documents and information for families, school procedures and policies, pictures of learning and school happenings, and information about school staff members. School websites can be a one-stop shop for families to quickly gain access to necessary information and the current happenings of the school community.

However, school websites often do not allow for families to provide feedback and ask clarifying questions. They are a repository of artifacts, information, and school events that help provide a window into the daily occurrences happening within the building. Most times, school websites serve as a means to communicate information rather than a means to engage in meaningful dialogue.

A third way schools can incorporate one-way communication is through the use of large-scale phone calls, e-mails, and text messages. Schools can quickly notify families with urgent updates regarding school closings or cancellations, upcoming events, or weekly updates by sending out one consistent message via phone, text, or e-mail to a large group of recipients all at one time.

This form of communication can be purchased through a third-party vendor or can be set up for free using a tool such as Remind (www.remind.com). The power of this type of communication is the ability to reach multiple recipients at one time so the same message can be heard or read at the same time. One way schools can use this messaging is by sending home a link to a weekly video to all families with updates for the

Figure 4.1.   First Grade Music Program

coming week using SafeShare (http://safeshare.tv/w/ziPGuSgCrl). Schools can also send home a prerecorded message over the weekend for their families with updates for the coming week.

One-way communication is important because it shares factual testimonials, important news and events, and necessary information in a timely, efficient manner. This information is intended to provide the necessary information for families to stay current with the news, events, and happenings within the school community.

Two-way communication is also important but serves a different purpose. Two-way communication options can lead to meaningful dialogue if used appropriately and effectively. Two-way communication tools allow for both sides of the communication aisle (schools and families) to have the opportunity to share information, ask questions, and learn from and with one another.

One high-tech example of two-way communication is through a school or classroom blog. School staff members can create a classroom blog, Facebook page, Shutterfly page, or other classroom site where information, events, and classroom happenings can be shared. The advantage of using these types of communication sites is in the opportunity that family members have to ask questions and learn alongside their students. These forms of two-way communication encourage families to be more engaged in their students' lives by providing opportunities for meaningful dialogue.

One low-tech example of two-way communication is through face-to-face meetings. These meetings could include a back-to-school night, parent orientation, parent-teacher conferences, student-led conferences, and curriculum nights, just to name a few. These face-to-face communications bring families into the building and classrooms so they can experience the learning firsthand. This form of two-way communication is one of the best ways to allow families the opportunity to view their child's experiences up close and personal.

The positive relationships that are established with school families and stakeholders provide the foundation for success. One-way and two-way communication tools can enhance communication and improve public relations while fostering positive relationships within the school community. Our world continues to evolve and change. As a result, we now have a multitude of ways to disseminate information and communication in a more efficient and cost-effective fashion.

It is important to remember to use every type of communication possible, as parents won't always have access to text messaging, e-mails, or social media tools. Schools need to have a variety of ways to communicate with their families. Schools should ask the following questions to determine the best methods of communication to meet the needs of their families and stakeholders. Where are your families and stakeholders?

Are they Twitter users? Is Facebook a platform they prefer? Or are they connected to social media at all?

We must answer these questions by soliciting feedback from our stakeholders. Doing so helps tell our stories of learning, shape the message we want our families to hear, and communicate effectively with diverse groups.

Ask stakeholders how they prefer to receive communication. This information will help focus in on the tools to use for communication. After determining the preferred communications vehicles for stakeholders, develop a differentiated menu of both one-way and two-way communication strategies to keep everyone engaged.

Creating a postcard like the one featured in Figure 4.2 to hand out to each family at the beginning of school provides that differentiated menu to share various methods of one-way and two-way communication in your school.

Whatever tools chosen to represent the message, use them and ask for feedback. Communication with the community is going to help bolster the appreciation it has for schools and learning, especially the schools connected to people's own neighborhoods. Be creative and adventurous when exploring new communication tools. Let not only the school know about these tools, but also let the district public relations professional know about the communication tools. It might be an opportunity for the whole district to incorporate some new ideas.

Welcome to Prairie Point Elementary School	
Three ways to help you connect with Prairie Point Elementary School	
1. Follow us on Twitter @PrairiePtElem and use #PioneerPride	2. Check our website for information, events and school happenings http://prairiepoint.parkhill.k12.mo.us/

3. Save the date!

Join us for coffee and our new family orientation
Thursday, August 13th in the Prairie Point Library

Figure 4.2.   Welcome to Prairie Point Elementary Postcard

Lastly, enjoy the process of communicating with school families. This should be a way to show personality, warmth, and spirit. Don't be afraid to let a bit of personality shine through a piece of communication. It makes educators relatable. And being relatable is the key to build relationships through communication.

SUMMARY

Communication encompasses opportunities for educators to have a conversation with the audience. Whether it's one-way or two-way communication, the message always has to be the same. The message has to be one of credibility and trust. Build relationships through communication. Sharpen the message of student achievement and polish it so that when you go out and communicate it, it sounds the same to everyone. Memorize your three main statements. Provide places for the audience to hear the message. Whatever medium fits the school culture, use it to showcase what the students are creating.

Make the context of education have an air of authority. The way educators communicate will dictate how the context gets received. Communicate professionally and with consistency in the message. This allows everyone to be school communicators. And these school communicators will be the ones helping distribute the message. With so many options for interaction, there is almost no excuse for not communicating in some organized fashion. Try something new — the parents of incoming kindergartners will most likely appreciate it. So will all the other stakeholders in your community.

FIVE

Social Media

Items to think about while reading this chapter:
Public relations point-of-view:

- How can both a school and a school district use social media to further their message?
- How does each school's message fit into the bigger picture?
- How to use Facebook, Twitter, and other social media tools.
- When social media becomes obsolete or not as prevalent, what will the next tool be to share your message?

Principal's point of view:

- Twitter, Voxer, Google+, and Facebook and how these work in schools.
- Using social media as ongoing professional development.
- How social media is flattening the walls of public education.

THE PUBLIC RELATIONS PROFESSIONAL

Social media. *Adweek* calls it an addiction. In fact, in *Adweek, The Huffington Post, Financial Times,* and *Yahoo News,* a web company called *GO-Globe* illustrates the impact of social media as shown in Table 5.1.

Also, according to *GO-Globe*:

- Users between the ages of fifteen and nineteen spend at least three hours a day on average on social media, while users between the ages of twenty and twenty-nine spend about two hours on their social media accounts.
- According to Facebook, the company's 1.32 billion users log in to the site for an average of seventeen minutes each day.

Table 5.1.

Social media platform	Active users (in billions)
Facebook	1,320
Google+	343
LinkedIn	300
Twitter	271
Tumblr	230

Source: "Social Media Addiction—Statistics and Trends." http://www.go-globe.com/blog/social-media-addiction/ (May 18, 2015).

- Eighteen percent of social media users can't go a few hours without checking Facebook.
- Sixteen percent of people rely on Twitter or Facebook for their morning news.
- More than 500 million tweets are sent out per day by users.
- The Google +1 button is pressed five billion times a day by users.
- LinkedIn signs on two new members every second.[1]

Social media is ingrained into its users' daily routine. It's part of a morning routine, a lunch routine, an afternoon routine, and an evening routine. The users between the ages of twenty and twenty-nine are the future parents in our schools. How do schools use social media to spread the message of student achievement?

As a school district, the message of achievement is the umbrella under which all the schools within the system are blanketed. This theme should resonate throughout the use of social media as well. The question is not *are you using social media?* The question is *how are you using social media?*

Using social media is another way to integrate a school's personal stories—but not just from the school's perspective. It invites interaction. It invites comments. It invites feedback. Social media allows everyone to join the conversation. It puts proponents (and naysayers) in the same arena and lets them publicly air their opinions. Some people get scared of this lack of control, but there are ways to respond and post that alleviate a sense of feeling overwhelmed.

Communications professionals should be the district-level educators responsible for overseeing social media in their school districts. Whether it's the Facebook account, Twitter feed, Instagram photos, Shutterfly album, Periscope video, YouTube channel, or Pinterest page, the communications professional should have direct oversight of the medium. This allows for a steady stream of messages that are linked and filtered through one voice. It's an avenue that will allow the audience to hear a consistent tone.

The tone should always remain professional and focused, but social media is one instance where it's sometimes appropriate to show a bit more fun, humor, or whimsy. Photos are the most viewed posts on Facebook for school and district pages. Parents and communities love seeing photos of activities and students. Just because it can be a bit more fun and whimsical though doesn't mean it loses its tone of student achievement. The posts, tweets, photos, and videos still have to show all the things that happen in schools surrounding achievement.

So if social media can be a bit more fun, a bit more relaxed, it means that the rules don't apply for spelling, grammar, and punctuation, right? Wrong. It is still a public and permanent etching on a school's identity. Because social media is quick and fluid, there is less time to follow the rules, but it almost makes it more important to be aware of them. Think about all the ramifications of a post or tweet. Even though it can be a bit more relaxed, it doesn't mean it can be lazy or thoughtless.

Consider a Facebook post of pictures of graduation. Have you inspected each photo for appropriateness? Consider a tweet of support for a local business. Have you considered the values and ethics of the business? Sometimes it can feel like we think about all the negative legal ramifications of social media, but if we are mindful of the potential ramifications without being too paralyzed by fear of the unknown, then social media becomes an important part of communicating the message.

Social media is like a little pickax, chiseling away at the audience. Each post or tweet or photo spread on social media is another outlet for small messages to be delivered. These small messages all contribute to the bigger picture. But just as small messages hammer away at the broader message, small messages can also blow up into broader messes.

The same procedures exist in sending out social media communication—think, review, think again, check for accuracy and tone, think again, then send. This little checklist can help avoid a disastrous post or tweet or photo. Another rule of thumb—ask yourself: would you be okay seeing your communication on the front page of a newspaper?

Not only is social media a chance to send out direct communication, it is also a chance for conversation and two-way communication in a public forum. Seeing interaction between numerous participants gives a good sense of what the vibe is for a certain topic, school, or proposal. The dialogue provides an immediate indication of positivity, indifference, or negativity. Constant attention to a school district's social media interactions will help with monitoring the perception of the audience.

Another way to use social media, and Twitter in particular, is to be up front about the stories happening in schools from the people inside the schools. It creates transparency from the people inside the system. This is what some refer to as crowdsourcing. It means that the people inside the schools are helping divide the responsibilities of communicating to the public. When teachers tweet about projects, students, classrooms, or ideas, they are helping tell the story of what happens in their schools.

As teachers jump on the Twitter train, they begin to be part of the story publicly. As a district communications professional, use that crowd to help spread your content. Have your teachers use a common hashtag to link all tweets about your schools. Then retweet (send the tweet again) to all of the people who follow your school district. Use the crowd to help make your content.

For example, if Red Bridge Elementary School sends a tweet like "look at all the #iweek projects—our students are roller coaster designers #centersd," then the communications professional should send that out to all the people who follow the school district's account. You've just used Red Bridge Elementary's tweet to create your message. Also notice how the hashtag *centersd* is used. This links all communication about the Center School District (centersd) to one common thread. Whoever searches for the hashtag *centersd* will see all the tweets about the school district.

Train teachers to use a district hashtag to link all their tweets about education. Train principals and central office administrators to use a district hashtag to link all their school and personal tweets. This guarantees content for your district audience directly from those working inside the schools. It's like a community forum without the coffee and donuts.

Something else that has been successful for some school districts using Twitter has been to establish district Twitter chats. Have someone from the school district (a savvy Twitter user) host a monthly tweet chat. Invite the teachers and staff to join in the conversation about a preselected topic during a preselected time. This becomes an interactive log of educators' thoughts and musings for anyone to see.

How does an educator feel about his school? Look at his tweets. How do lots of educators in the same school district feel about their schools? Look at their organized Twitter chats. It shows personality, it shows dedication, it shows humanity, and it shows how the people within an organization think about the mission they are working on. Educators all over the world are tweeting about their schools and classrooms; just consolidate the thoughts of your own school district under a common hashtag and be amazed at what they are saying.

Also think about Twitter as professional development. Educators say that Twitter has provided them some of the most relevant professional development in which they get to participate. Twitter is where educators are going to feel connected to other educators who think about the same things. It's a medium for educators to feel connected to someone in their school district or someone halfway around the world. Educators get to choose this form of professional development, and this choice reflects who they are.

Every day is a test of who you are. Every day is a test of how you present yourself to the world (colleagues, students, parents). By choosing professional activities that engage, stretch, and challenge yourself, it forces growth and learning. An activity like Twitter that produces real-time thoughts and content from a single person becomes a log of what that person thinks and dreams. It shows what the user is working on, being challenged by, or interacting with. The tweets become an image of the person and the entity. It builds a brand. It builds a perception. It tests (measures) what people think of educators and schools.

The communications professional should put her arms around all of these educator tweets, hold them close, study them, and then rerelease them into her school community through her district's account. Then she should wrap her arms around parent posts, community leader posts, student posts, and anyone else commenting on her school district; study them; and then release those as well. The job is about using the people connected to the school district to help spread the message.

Social media encompasses so many outlets, it's difficult to cover all of them in a chapter. The gist is that social media can be used to help spread small messages and large messages. Every social media encounter matters to the larger perception of an organization or person. Use it to build an online presence for an audience to view. Use it to build a brand.

Social media not only showcases what educators do for a school; it also enhances the perception of public education in our country. It becomes a conglomeration of educators whispering all the good things happening in our schools. It becomes a barrage of voices chiseling away at what it means to be better for students and the community. It's a chance to be heard, seen, and understood.

And even when the mentioned social media tools start becoming outdated or replaced with other new technological mediums and sharing sites, the fundamental rules of what to share and how to share it will remain the same. There will still remain the need for an inundation of messages about student achievement and the impact of our schools.

We will always have ways to communicate the message; the challenge continues to be figuring out the best way to do so. Take a chance on something new—because there will always be something new to try.

THE PRINCIPAL

Imagine you had a question and could talk to twenty people to get help in answering your question. Not bad, right? Now imagine asking hundreds or thousands of individuals the same question. Much better, right? The idea of disconnected teachers working in silos is becoming less and less of a reality.

With the advancement of social media, teachers have the ability to connect with other like-minded educators across the country and the world. Teachers have the ability to ask questions and receive immediate answers and feedback from different perspectives. Teachers have the ability to expand their personal learning network (PLN) to find new ways to provide engaging, relevant learning experiences for their students.

Social media is a valuable tool that can help change the landscape in education. Social media is flattening the walls of education by opening up new opportunities in which to learn and grow. Social media can and should be used in a variety of ways to change how schools and professional development are viewed: for ongoing professional development and for transparent two-way communication between schools and the larger school community.

Traditionally, professional development for staff has consisted of school staff meetings, grade-level or department team meetings, district trainings, or attending a conference. While none of these options are bad options, it limits the number of people who can participate in the staff development due to location or cost.

Social media is changing the way that professional development can happen in schools. Through the use of social media tools such as Facebook, Twitter, Voxer, Google Hangouts, and Periscope, professional development can look different and provide unique experiences that traditional professional development may not offer. One of the main advantages of social media sites is the constant availability and connection they offer. These sites are available to use on computers, phones, tablets, and some gaming devices, allowing connectivity in virtually any location.

One social media tool that might not be thought of as a professional development tool is Facebook. Most people use Facebook as a way to connect with friends, see pictures of relatives, and play Candy Crush and other games. However, Facebook is one social media avenue for ongoing professional development.

Facebook offers the opportunity to create groups focusing on a common interest or topic. Members of that group can post articles, links, videos, and other supplementary materials. Facebook allows information sharing on a wall for others to see. Schools could create Facebook pages geared around a topic and have members contribute. For example, if a staff is focusing on developing a growth mindset for student and adult learners, a Facebook page could be created, and staff members could join, hold conversations, and share resources and ideas that could be accessed at any time.

Twitter is another social media tool that presents ongoing professional development opportunities. Twitter allows users to compose tweets up to 140 characters that appear on the Twitter feed and are visible by anyone who follows the user. These tweets can include pictures, links, and videos.

One of the unique features to Twitter is the use of a hashtag (#). A hashtag acts as a filter and/or a tag to identify and classify tweets. For example, if a twitter user wanted to designate that a tweet was about writing, the user could use *#writing* at the end of the tweet and anyone who searched *#writing* would see that tweet.

An added benefit of using hashtags is that it allows the user to follow a conversation occurring in real time. Many participants who attend conferences use a hashtag so they can learn from other participants and share their learning with one another. Twitter users can virtually attend a conference by following the hashtag and learning alongside those participants physically in attendance.

Educators routinely participate in education chats hosted on Twitter. In these chats, questions are asked by a Twitter user or moderator and other participants respond using the chat hashtag. These chats occur throughout the day, in the evenings, and on weekends and allow Twitter users the chance to grow and learn from and with one another on a variety of topics. The chat topics can be content specific (#mathchat, #sciencechat, #sschat, #writingchat), grade-level specific (#kinderchat, #1stchat, #5thchat), topic specific (#atplc, #edtech, #growthmindset), or day specific (#satchat, #satchatwc, #sunchat). The benefit of these chats is they are a live and interactive form of professional development.

Voxer is yet another form of professional development educators can use to connect with other educators. Voxer is similar to a walkie-talkie type device and provides live and recorded voice, text, pictures, and video all in one app. Unlike Twitter, which is limited to 140 characters, Voxer does not have a limit on the amount of time or number of characters. Users send a *vox* and can ask questions, listen live as users respond, or listen later when it is more convenient for the user and then choose to save, forward, or star a vox.

Voxer allows a depth of connection that Twitter does not allow because longer conversations with individuals or groups can occur at one time. It allows staff members to have book studies from their living room couches. Staff members can all read a book and then discuss the book from their homes. Additionally, the Voxer chat is saved so users can revisit the discussion at a later time if they would like.

Finally, Periscope and Google Hangouts on Air are other social media sites or apps that allow live streaming video to occur. Periscope allows broadcasters the ability to share video and audio with their viewers either publically or privately. A broadcaster simply sends out a tweet with the link to the broadcast and viewers can view the event through the eyes of the broadcaster. Viewers can interact with the broadcaster in real time, using messaging.

Periscope offers a world of potential for professional development. Periscope can be used during a staff meeting to allow staff members who are not present the opportunity to watch the meeting. It can be used at conferences to allow the conference sessions to be transmitted to nonparticipants so they can experience the conference as well. Or it can be used by a teacher to record her teaching and review it within a twenty-four-hour window to reflect upon her teaching and lesson effectiveness. Periscope can open up the walls by providing live streaming of events that could positively affect the learning and professional development of educators.

Similarly, Google Hangouts on Air can provide streaming capabilities for a staff meeting to allow staff members who are not present the opportunity to watch the meeting. Google Hangouts on Air can be used at conferences to allow the conference sessions to be transmitted to nonparticipants so they can experience the conference too. The hangouts can be used by a teacher to record her teaching and upload it to YouTube to again reflect upon her teaching and lesson effectiveness.

By uploading the video to YouTube, the video can be viewed outside a twenty-four-hour window to provide additional opportunities for review and reflection. Google Hangouts on Air, like Periscope, can open up the walls of a conference or classroom by providing live streaming of events that can positively affect the learning and professional development of educators.

In addition to social media being used for professional development, social media can be used as another form of communication with the larger school community. Schools can create Facebook, Twitter, Voxer, and Periscope accounts. These social media sites provide a window into the daily learning occurring in schools.

Many schools have Facebook pages where families and community members can get updates on school happenings and events, view current information, and view pictures and videos from classroom and school learning experiences. Facebook allows the larger school community to have a central location to connect with one another.

Schools can use Twitter accounts to share pictures of learning occurring in the classrooms and tweet out updates and timely information such as school closings, delays, events, and other time-sensitive information. Schools can also use Twitter and create a school-specific hashtag such as #eaglepride or #pioneerpride to help users search for tweets more easily.

Periscope could be used to live-stream special events for schools. Music programs, graduations, awards assemblies, or PTA meetings could all be streamed live using the Periscope app to provide another opportunity for the larger school community to be a part of the school events without having to be physically present.

Social media offers opportunities for educators to connect, grow, and learn with other educators outside the walls of their school, their district, their state, and even their country. Social media allows educators the chance to connect with others in an effort to flatten the walls of education in the ever-changing global society. Additionally, social media allows schools to connect with the larger school community by providing a level of transparency and openness with school learning, events, and activities in a real-time fashion. Best of all, all of these social media sites are apps found on almost all smartphones so that families, staff, students, and community members have instant access to the latest news, happenings, and events.

SUMMARY

Social media is an addiction. It is part of its users' routine. Learning to grab the social media bull by the horns and use it as a way to talk to your audience is an evolving communication medium. Use social media to show a bit of fun and whimsy in your communication while still maintaining an overarching theme of student achievement and professionalism.

Use social media to create small moments and small pictures of what happens in schools. Use it to create an immediate source of professional development for educators. Use it to create a conversation. All of these posts, tweets, instagrams, or voxes point attention in education's direction. It creates connection between the user and the disseminator. It creates a wanted connection because the user seeks it out.

Every social media encounter matters to the larger perception of an organization or person. Use it to build an online persona for your schools or yourself. Use it to build a brand.

Open the walls of the classroom and show the audience what learning looks like. Social media can help accomplish this. Let users help spread the message and paint the pictures of what we want everyone to know and see in education.

NOTE

1. "Social Media Addiction – Statistics and Trends." http://www.go-globe.com/blog/social-media-addiction/ (May 18, 2015).

SIX

Events and Activities

Items to think about while reading this chapter:
Public relations point of view:

- Running school events and activities.
- What purpose do your events and activities serve?
- How do they usher in a sense of belonging and connectedness to the school and community?

Principal's point of view:

- Activities bring the school and community together.
- Events need to be focused on school's goals—don't just have an event because you're supposed to.
- What is the purpose? Who will this benefit?
- How will this make our school better?

THE PUBLIC RELATIONS PROFESSIONAL

Everything a school produces contributes to its brand. Whether it's a test, a banner, students, teachers, or an event, each of these things is a reflection of the school district and the community. Events and activities might be the biggest showcase that people get to experience when visiting a school. Think of school events as showcases of an experience. An event is a chance to host guests and provide a welcoming experience to any person who attends.

When someone comes to your personal home for a cup of tea (or other beverage), a birthday party, movie night, or whatever the occasion might be, there exists some planning and preparation of your house beforehand. Cleaning, arranging, thinking, cooking, mowing, planting. All these actions are transferable to schools as well. Think about hosting an event at school just as you would think about hosting an event at your home. Hospitality should extend to schools as it would in a home. The art of inviting the community into the front door of their proverbial school home should be tended to thoughtfully.

Just as the experience of an event at a home dictates the perception of comfort and love, the experience of an event at school should dictate a perception of comfort, thought, neatness, cleanliness, and care. Remember, snap judgments are going to be made even before a guest enters the school. What is the perception the school is promoting?

Bypass any chance for a guest to make a negative judgment about a school even before the event or activity begins. Make sure the look of the school is so good that guests comment on the excellence of the facility or don't comment at all because the facility is as it is expected to be. Don't give people a chance to criticize how a school looks. That is the first barrier to overcome without even starting an event or activity.

Well-run events and activities start on time, are conducted efficiently, and have a sense of purpose. By now it's been established that the message is about student achievement, and this message still applies to events and activities. Is the curriculum night helping parents and community patrons understand the curriculum or understand the message that students at school work toward academic standards that help them prepare for life after high school? It's both, but school leaders should always make the connection back to why they are hosting the event.

How about starting the event with introductions and then adding a sentence or two as to why the event is important for student achievement? Could a student be the one to introduce the event? It sounds simple and easy enough, but the intentional phrasing of purpose (and even having students begin the event) can continually affect how parents, community patrons, students, and staff feel about the academic climate of a school. *Welcome to Center Middle School. We are grateful to you for joining us this evening at our eighth-grade recognition ceremony. I'm Ms. Williams, the principal of Center Middle School, and we are here this evening to honor our students in their accomplishments of achievement in math, reading, writing, and the arts. Tonight we celebrate their performance, hard work, and dedication to making our school a place of achievement and excellence. And to the parents and guardians in attendance this evening, thank you for supporting our students in this endeavor.*

The five sentences accomplish introduction, message of achievement, and gratitude. Set the expectation that every time the school hosts an event or activity, the occasion is going to be professional and purposeful. This is where principals are so important to helping set the tone for expectation in a school. Running an event is setting the expectation for how guests are going to be treated each time they enter the school.

How much pride is invested in your school? This sense of pride should be a driver of the experience people have when attending an event or walking in to drop off their child. How will a guest know if a school takes pride in itself? By the appearance, the attitude, the timeliness, the message, and the overall sense of experience when interacting with that school. Pick the low-hanging fruit. What's easy to change and affect? Start with the simple things like appearance and message, and then grow to incorporate the attitude and the experience. These changes are quick, but it takes time to nurture them and continually focus on them.

The goal is that school events and activities extend the school day into showcases of student achievement. Whether academics, music, art, or sports, activities should promote the message that student talent comes in many forms. Student talent can also be fun. And emotional. And intense. And lighthearted. And visionary. And prideful. All these emotions are involved in student activities and events. Schools understand that even through the seriousness of student achievement, there is also fun and emotion wrapped up in what children experience at school.

Make the events and activities at school highlight what's special about the students and staff who inhabit the hallways. Maybe it's a charity basketball game between teachers and students to raise money for a student trip to astronaut camp. Maybe it's a talent show that showcases student and teacher talent in the musical arts. Maybe it's a recognition ceremony to honor the students who've passed certain benchmarks. There's always a reason to celebrate. Even the smallest accomplishments can be big events for some students. Use events and activities to celebrate student achievement in whatever form highlights a specific school's special talent.

Then take that event or activity opportunity to reiterate the message of achievement and give a perception of pride, appearance, and quality. Make people feel connected to the purpose. Usher in a sense of connection to school and to the community.

THE PRINCIPAL

Schools are often seen as a gathering place where learning occurs, families connect, memories are made, fun is had, and the community comes together. For some towns, the school is the center of the community. For other towns, the school is the center of the neighborhood. Regardless of the physical location, schools are frequently the central locale where communities connect, bond, and grow.

Schools have many different types of events that aim to bring the school and community together. School events allow the community to get a glimpse of the learning and the impact it has on the students, their families, and the community as a whole. These events can range from PTA meetings, to back-to-school nights, to music programs, to student-led conferences, to holiday events, to athletic events, to informational events. The events and activities that happen outside the school hours serve as a connection between school and the community.

But how do schools go about determining the number and types of events they have for the community? Are events scheduled because they have always been scheduled or are they being scheduled because they meet a goal for the school? Focus on a few key, aligned events that will create a powerful connection and provide value to guests' time.

Many hours are spent putting events together, and it feels terrible to have underwhelming attendance. To value the time of the planners and the time of the community members, have a process to determine whether an event should be developed to benefit the larger school community as a whole. Using a model like plan, do, study, act (PDSA) can help guide the process and help to ensure the cycle of continual improvement is being used each year for each event. When planning school events, three questions should help steer the process:

- What is the purpose of this event?
- Who will this event benefit?
- How does this event align with our school goals and make our school better?

Take the first question, "What is the purpose of this event?" Schools should not just have an event because they are supposed to. The event needs to have a clear focus and goal in mind. As schools write their building school improvement plans (BSIPs), are there any action steps about involving families and communities in the learning process? Are these key stakeholders being addressed and included in the learning process? If not, including the families and community members should be addressed as part of the BSIP.

When examining the purpose of events and activities, a three-step process can be used to determine the intended purpose. First, brainstorm answers to the question, "Why are we having this event?" This simple question can help steer the event and provide clarity for the purpose of the event. If the planning committee cannot clearly answer this question, perhaps the event is not needed or simply needs refinement.

The second step involves examining what is to be accomplished with the event. Brainstorm a list of intended outcomes and use the ideas to help plan the event. If an intended outcome is to have a large turnout from the community, what steps do the planners take to publicize and promote the event? If an intended outcome is to learn about the curriculum and provide an overview of learning to come this year, what is necessary so that the community hears a similar message throughout the event? This second step allows schools to begin to define the details necessary for a successful event.

The third step is to share the ideas with other stakeholders. Typically, a planning committee heads up the process of planning these events and the event falls on the creative minds and shoulders of a select few. Take the proposed ideas and answers to the key questions listed above to other groups to gain their insight and perspective. These groups could include additional staff members, students, parents, and community members. Using the resources and perspectives of all key stakeholders will allow for an event to better meet the needs of the school and the community.

After a clear purpose for the event has been established, turn the focus to the second question, "Who will this event benefit?" This question serves as a guide to ensure that all community members are included in the event. Will the event be in the morning when working parents will not be able to attend? Will this event have a cost associated with it that will alienate certain groups?

For some community members, school was not a place full of fond memories. This may cause some people to not want to come to school to support the event. Having an understanding of this and working to break down these barriers is crucial to the success of an event. How can schools create a welcoming environment so that the community wants to attend?

Have students take on leadership roles at these events to draw reluctant families into events. What family does not want to show up and be proud of their son or daughter who is greeting people at the door? What family does not want to show up and be proud of their son or daughter who is the emcee of the event? What family does not want to show up and be proud of their son or daughter who is presenting at the event? By incorporating students in leadership roles at events, family members are more likely to attend.

Not all school events need to occur at school. If the intended audience is one particular subgroup of students who live in one particular area of town, perhaps the school event should go to them and meet them at a convenient location. Enrollment clinics could happen at various apartment complexes in which it is a struggle for families from those complexes to physically get to school to enroll. After-school tutoring could occur at the local community center or neighborhood clubhouse to draw more students in so they don't have to worry about transportation. Schools could distribute summer survival kits to neighborhoods at the start of summer. The ideas are endless of how school events can occur outside school walls and in the community to better serve student and family needs.

Once the goal or purpose of the event has been clearly established and the intended audience has been identified, schools must look at how the event aligns with school goals and ask *how will this make our school better?* Will this event create a stronger sense of school pride? Will this event allow more people to see the learning occurring in our school and help tell our story? Will this event get more people through our doors so we can better develop relationships?

If schools can clearly identify and articulate how an event will make their school better, it is worth having. If schools cannot clearly articulate how an event will make their school better, perhaps other questions need to be revisited for clarity.

Once an event has occurred, it is important to study the results before the next event is planned. Schools should gather feedback on the success of the event as close to the completion of the event as possible. There are many technology tools, such as Google Forms or SurveyMonkey, that can help facilitate this process. When designing the survey questions, incorporate the goals and provide opportunities for attendees to comment on the goals to judge the effectiveness of the event. Figure 6.1 is an example of how to gather feedback tied to the goals of the event.

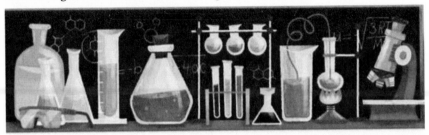

Science Fair

A goal for the science fair was to allow students the opportunity to share their investigations with the school community. On a scale of 1 to 5, was this goal accomplished?

1 2 3 4 5

Did not successfully meet the goal ◎ ◎ ◎ ◎ ◎ Successfully met the goal

What specific ways can we improve our efforts in meeting this goal?

Figure 6.1.

Surveys incorporating specific, targeted questions will help schools determine the overall effectiveness of the event, gather ideas for future events, and involve more stakeholders in the evaluation aspect of the event.

Now that the event has been planned, the event has occurred, and the results of the event have been studied, make appropriate plans for the next event. The benefit of asking for specific, targeted feedback is to allow stakeholders to share what went well and ideas for improvement. This data will allow schools to modify events to better align to the goals and meet the needs of the community. Take time at the completion of the event to gather feedback and create action steps for the next event. The event will be fresh in the minds of the school and the feedback will serve to create better experiences for future events.

School events, either at school or in the community, are powerful examples of ways schools and communities can work together to support one another. Schools need the support of the community to be successful, and the community sees the school as a central hub where connections and community bonding occurs.

SUMMARY

Plan events and activities that allow schools to highlight the continued message of student achievement. Think of events as an opportunity to invite guests into your home and showcase your hospitality. Plan with purpose and make schools the hub of the community through events and activities.

Celebrate and connect through the events hosted at school. Invite students to help plan and participate in school events and activities. Welcome feedback and try new ideas, always keeping the focus on achievement and celebration. Make the events and activities hosted by your school a piece of building relationships with the community.

SEVEN

The Community

Items to think about while reading this chapter:
Public relations point of view:

- Schools are the foundation of the community.
- Schools and community are codependent when thinking about public education.
- Bad schools equal an undesirable neighborhood.
- Good schools equal a desirable neighborhood.
- How do schools fit into their community?
- How does public relations help support the cause?

Principal's point of view:

- Tap into resources in the community—guest speakers, focus groups, a volunteer program.
- How can you partner with the community to create win-win scenarios?
- Ask *what does the community want out of graduates?*
- How schools can support what the community wants.

THE PUBLIC RELATIONS PROFESSIONAL

Schools are the bridges to connecting communities. Schools link people together. Think about this example: in an administrative meeting to recap the school year, the principals and district-level administrators are discussing a SWOT (strengths, weaknesses, opportunities, threats) analysis encompassing four different areas of vision for the school district. The four overarching areas are culture (sense of community, family), achievement (curriculum, growth, learning), resources, and equity.

The portion of the time devoted to culture and community seemed to take the most time. Why? Because this is where the discussion focuses on the stories of how important the community is in supporting the work of schools. The leaders feel like a huge win for the year is the fact that the community is involved in the vision and mission of the schools. The leaders understand that the community supports what they are doing to raise kids into successful young adults.

The example illustrates the human science behind how emotionally linked people are to feeling a sense of belonging. Communities create a sense of belonging. Schools play an important role in creating that sense of community and belonging. Schools help people identify with a certain community. Schools and communities are almost interchangeable in how they are viewed. Good schools equal good communities and bad schools equal bad communities. If that's true, then it becomes the schools' responsibility to ensure the community works on being better. And it's also true, then, that the community's responsibility becomes ensuring the schools work on being better. It goes both ways.

It's a codependent relationship. It's interchangable—schools are communities and communities are schools.

Public relations professionals can help shape this relationship. The influence of the public relations professional should reach beyond the confines of the schools and homes of the students she serves. The influence should reach into the town, city, state, and country. This happens by equating the work of schools as the work of everyone. Education is everyone's job, and public relations helps convey that notion.

Schools should think about how to continually make what happens in schools (student achievement) part of what the community knows and supports. Community can mean several things, but in general, this community is made up of people with direct connections to your schools (students, teachers, parents), people who live within your school district boundaries, and people who live in the surrounding areas. It also means businesses, politicians, parks and recreation, home associations, faith organizations, community centers, and an array of other entities that have a stake in the success of a community. This community should know what happens with student achievement in schools.

A sense of community requires work from both sides—from the community side and the school side. Both should be pushing on each other to create some tension on the system. This tension is what provides the inspiration and motivation to continue pushing for growth and achievement.

Bringing people from the community into schools is a way to bridge the knowledge gap to help patrons understand what happens in their community schools. Having people in the community see and be part of the school and what the students are learning creates a firsthand experience for patrons. Whether volunteers, career day guest speakers, business partners, restaurant owners, politicians, moms and dads, grandparents, or other educators, all of the people entering school have to feel a sense of being part of something special.

Something special doesn't have to mean this magical place where rainbows and sunshine are constantly making sparkling lights all over the school, but it does mean that a special place is somewhere where people feel like there is honorable and good work happening with kids. Special places have everyday miracles of growing kids into solid learners, and they also have real challenges of making sure kids are served well even if they didn't have breakfast, a clean shirt, or a parent supporting them at home. Creating a sense of community in which guests can enter a school and see and feel the vibe of togetherness and sense of purpose is where the magic happens.

When the inside of a school is functioning at a high level of community, then it's easier to project that function out into the community. As educators, the message of community is both inside the school walls and outside in the neighborhoods and city. Trying to always convey that to teachers and students is part of a good leader's responsibility. Educators have a duty to the community.

Good educators feel this sense of duty and responsibility to the community. They get part of their mission from the community, meaning good educators translate the importance of serving their community into their message to internal constituents and outside patrons. Good educators tell their audience why school is important to the community.

In the message, educators have to remember that their influence goes beyond where they think it will go. Inspiring people is part of the job requirement. Make a sense of community part of the inspiration to go out and do good work. The good work will come back in the form of support, transparency, and collaboration. All of these intangibles have an impact on student learning. These feelings of support, transparency, and collaboration create a two-way flow of dependency that boosts all those involved.

Public relations takes these notions of community connection and helps filter partnerships, stories, CEO guest speakers, community organizations, churches, whatever through the lens of one mission. When we look through the lens of community connection, we begin to realize the ways in which we all share the same mission. *Public relations* unites causes and points people in the same direction.

Pay attention to how schools and educators relate to the community. Make it part of the mission to understand the responsibility schools have to the people and organizations in the community. The link between community and school is built through relationships. Tend to the relationships and nurture the partnerships. And remember, good schools are part of good communities.

THE PRINCIPAL

Public education consists of hardworking individuals who care about learning. Businesses want a workforce that is equipped with a wide range of skills and the ability to apply learning across multiple modalities. How can schools and businesses develop a partnership to help all students learn and be prepared for college, career, and life? There are some important steps to help schools and the community form strategic partnerships for the advancement and betterment of student learning.

The first step in building a strategic partnership between schools and the community is to determine the needs of both entities. What do schools need in this strategic alignment? What do schools hope to accomplishment by creating an alliance with the community? What does the community want out of recent graduates? What can schools do to support these needs from businesses? Determining the needs is essential to maximize the relationship and effectively serve both parties well.

Schools should begin this process by determining the skills and abilities the community looks for in recent graduates. Determining the skill set of future graduates can be done through surveys, collaborative meetings, and developing internships and community partnerships. The time invested up front in understanding the needs of the community and businesses, will help schools better identify and understand ways to continue to provide an educational opportunity to all students that will prepare them for college, career, and life.

Schools should advertise their desire to continue to develop the skill set of graduates to provide opportunities for students to be better prepared for the experiences that await them after high school. Schools can invite various business and community leaders to participate in roundtable discussions focusing on specific skills needed in different professions. If schools take the time to listen and gather input as to the skill sets needed to be successful in today's business world, universities, and community environments, schools can begin to determine if the learning experiences provided to students are serving the needs of the larger community.

The second step for schools is to determine their own needs, based partly on the feedback of the community. When schools examine the curriculum, the four Cs (creativity, collaboration, communication, and critical thinking), and the strengths of teaching staffs in conjunction with a chart like the one shown in Table 7.1, they can help identify strengths and any potential gaps.

Schools can fill in the left column with the skills identified by the businesses, colleges, and community members. Next, schools can determine if and where these skills are addressed in the intended curriculum, educational opportunities for the four Cs both in and out of the classroom within the larger school setting, and if any teaching staff members have

Table 7.1.

	Intended curriculum	Opportunities for the 4 C's in and out of the classroom (creativity, collaboration, communication, and critical thinking)	Strengths of teaching staff (identify specific teaching staff)
Skill #1			
Skill #2			
Skill #3			

clearly identified strengths with these skills. The benefit of this chart consists in the ability to clearly identify areas of strength and areas for growth based on the current reality of the skills and the educational opportunity.

Once schools have worked collaboratively to identify the needs of businesses, colleges, and the community and clearly identified where in the educational program these skills are addressed, the focus can be on identifying talented individuals both connected and not connected to the school who can provide relevant, authentic experiences for the students. If schools were to look at the various fields that school families are associated with, the list of differing professions would be quite large.

Professions of the families in our schools include police officers and firefighters, marketing directors, authors, city council members, medical professionals, attorneys, educators, professional athletes, skilled laborers, and many more. So how do schools tap into this knowledge base and skill set?

At the elementary level and middle school levels, schools can provide career share days for their families and students. Family members sign up to come and speak to students about their professions, the skills needed to get to the position they currently are in, and how school has helped them achieve their goals. Providing an opportunity to get family members into the school is important. Having events such as "donuts with dudes" or "muffins with moms" and then asking family members to come and speak to classes at a later date in the school year is an efficient way to have them sign up while spending time and eating donuts and muffins with their children.

In addition to having families come in and share their professions and the training required for their jobs, elementary schools often invite community members to tell historical stories, show artifacts, and share traditions of multiple generations. One example of the partnership forged between schools and the community is by having a Veteran's Day fireside chat. Members of the military are invited into school on Veteran's Day, and the students ask questions to learn about their service, life in the military, and the tour of duty. These fireside chats allow community members and family members a chance to tell their story to today's students and keep alive the rich tradition and stories passed down from generation to generation. The community members enjoy the opportunity to come and share their stories, and the students enjoy the experience of learning from our veterans through the veterans' experiences.

At the high school level, schools can provide opportunities for students to listen to guest speakers and then work to establish opportunities for students to observe, shadow, and intern in various professional settings. These observations, shadowing experiences, and internships help students better understand the skills necessary for the profession and might help solidify a career path for students.

Another example of what schools can use to partner with the community is by developing a volunteer program to fit the needs of the students and school. The volunteer program can and should look different based on the needs of each school district. The roles of volunteers can include classroom assistant, mentor, business partner, tutor, or gardener to help in school beautification efforts. There are a number of roles volunteers can play, and they provide skills that are essential to the overall success of school communities.

To help volunteers be used effectively and efficiently, the following steps can be established to provide a consistent message and training for all volunteers:

1. Volunteers complete a background check to be kept on file in the school or district office in accordance with board policies.
2. Volunteers should attend an orientation or training where the volunteer role is more clearly defined and explained. Volunteers will have the opportunity to ask questions and gain a better understanding of the school's or district's needs.
3. Volunteers will complete an interest survey selecting the types of volunteer experiences in which they would like to share their talents and identify the levels of students they would like to work with when volunteering.
4. Volunteers work with the volunteer coordinator, either at the district or building level, to determine the times volunteering will occur and the types of volunteering experiences to be shared.
5. The volunteer coordinator will remain in contact with the volunteers to answer any questions or to provide guidance to provide a positive volunteer experience for all students, staff, and volunteers.

The key to building partnerships with businesses, colleges, and the community is understanding how to tap into resources in the community—

guest speakers, focus groups, and volunteer programs. The talent, experience, and knowledge exists within the communities; schools just need to find creative ways to partner with these entities to allow students real-world, relevant learning experiences to prepare them for college, career, and life.

SUMMARY

Schools and communities are interlinked. Both are dependent on the other for success.

Make it part of your mission to understand the responsibility you have to the people and organizations in your community. The connection between community and school relies on relationships. Nurture the relationship.

Find ways to invite the community to help shape student growth. Whether through volunteers or parents or business partners, there are countless ways to solicit help. Outside community members need to see what you are doing in schools. They need to be part of the learning experiences of our students.

And remember, good schools are part of good communities. And good communities are part of good schools.

EIGHT

Your Brand

Items to think about while reading this chapter:
Public relations point of view:

- People make up the brand.
- A school will take on the persona of the principal, teachers, and students. Hence, it's important for the people to be good brand ambassadors for their school.
- Public relations paints a picture of schools and their people.
- The brand is that one snapshot that flashes in your mind about a particular school.
- Singular moments combine to form that image. Those small moments add up to large pictures in our catalog of thoughts about schools. Make the moments revolve around the brand you want to evoke.
- Is it professionalism? Is it academics? Is it emotional? Is it rigor? Is it love? Maybe it's all of those things, but choose to focus on a brand that promotes a culture of learning and high achievement.

Principal's point of view:

- We have to find a way to tell our story (what do we want those outside our walls to know?).
- If we don't tell our story, someone else will.
- What do we want our school to be known for?
- Getting everyone on the same page with what we want the school to feel and look like.

THE PUBLIC RELATIONS PROFESSIONAL

Everyone in the community helps shape the brand and image for where kids, young and old, go to learn and grow each day. These buildings where kids stream in and out and move throughout a mass of other kids and teachers and administrators and parents are the hallowed ground where futures are built. These devoted and sacred places hold precious responsibility within their walls. The iconic picture of an old schoolhouse with kids running through the schoolyard still elicits a feeling of goodness, charm, and childhood.

And even as the old schoolhouse can make the best of us yearn for childhood and innocence, and even as the picture has changed from an old one-room wood structure to a modern glass-windowed, steel, stone, and brick mainstay, there still exists an overwhelmingly nostalgic and positive view of schools. The brand of schools is still good, but it has to continue getting better and modernized to compete with the influx of outside interests and wary parents. The brand continues to be built one dream at a time.

Superintendents are the brand. Public relations professionals are the brand. Principals are the brand. Teachers are the brand. Parents are the brand. And students are the brand. The kind, grade, or make of a product is the brand. What kind of educators are working in our schools? What grade of students are learning in our schools? What are our people made of? This is the stuff of branding. In schools, the people make up the brand.

The kind, grade, or make of schools contributes to how people feel about a school system. The brand contributes to how people feel about education. And the people are the kind, grade, and make of a school. Those connected to the schools are the brand of the schools. Within schools, because education is about kids, shaping a brand based on those students and people who interact with them is the way to go. A school will take on the persona of the principal, teachers, and students. Hence, it's important for the people to be good brand ambassadors for their school. Bottom line: the people working in schools have to be able to be the face of public education, and the students have to understand their role in being brand ambassadors. The adults and kids have to be honorable, ethical, hardworking, and tough do-gooders to be able to be the face public education needs.

If people are going to be part of the brand, then ensure that the educators connected to schools and the students in those schools know their role in being brand ambassadors. Do they know the message? Do they know the feeling that the mission is supposed to cause? This is where public relations contributes to spreading the feelings of what happens in schools to those outside their walls. Public relations shows the public what the brand is.

Public relations paints a picture of schools and their people. If we are trying to form and show a picture of our schools, the brand is that one snapshot that flashes in the audience's mind about a particular school. Singular moments combine to form that image. And those small moments add up to large pictures in our catalog of thoughts about schools.

Make the moments you share with the audience revolve around the feelings that you want to evoke. Those moments will build your brand.

Is the feeling one of professionalism? Is it academics? Is it emotion? Is it rigor? Is it love? Maybe it's all of those things, but choose to focus on a brand and a feeling that promote a culture of learning and high achievement. Almost all emotions we have can be linked to feelings about schools. Schools produce all kinds of feelings of joy, pride, success, growth, anger, sadness, inspiration, frustration, and happiness. Use those feelings to sell the brand you want to the public to buy.

Then take those feelings and show the public the range of emotion that education stirs up. Stir up the positive emotions more frequently. Figures 8.1 to 8.8 show some tweets from people in the education arena that in less than 140 characters make the reader feel emotional about school.

 CSD_Athletics @bsweeten1 · 20h
This is why we coach. " Thank you for always being there when I need you and loving me like a son happy Father's Day" #centersd

Figure 8.1. CSD Athletics Tweet

 Kelly Wachel @KellyWachel · Jun 1
Advice for next year's middle schoolers from current students. Already prepping! Carry on! #centersd

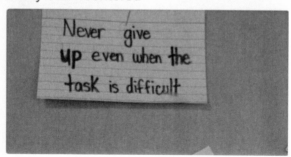

Figure 8.2. Kelly Wachel Tweet

Ashley DeSandre @peteach58 · May 14
My favorite part of Center graduation! #Classof2015 #Family
#MoreHugsThanHandshakes @CenterSD

Figure 8.3.   Ashley DeSandre Tweet

 Christopher Kohm @JacketTennis · Jun 17
Playing with sand and creating the physical features of Africa. Too much fun.
#CenterSD

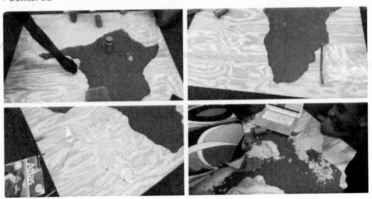

Figure 8.4.   Christopher Kohm Tweet

Katy Liechti @artfullydelish · Jun 15
Henry's first Twitter chat #centersd #BabyFirsts thanks @robynholsman for hosting!

Figure 8.5.   Katy Liechti Tweet

Tyler Shannon @TSHANNON49 · Jun 15
A6 If we practice GRACE w/ our Ss they will practice GRACE w/ their Ts #CenterSD

Figure 8.6.   Tyler Shannon Tweet

Katelyn Isom @IsomKatelyn · Feb 19
Sneak peek of some amazing student work for the first major project in Digital Arts! #centerSD #center58art

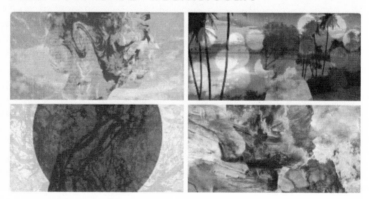

Figure 8.7.   Katelyn Isom Tweet

Drnibbelink @drnibbelink · Jun 13

Center School Board recognized by MO
School Board Assoc for Leadership in
Teaching, Learning and Assessment
#centersd

Figure 8.8.   Dr. Nibbelink Tweet

Love, never give up, fun, hugs, babies, grace, magic, art, leadership, teaching, and learning. They all go together and they all describe what the educational world provides in our lives. These firsthand accounts of what school means to these people are not unlike what school means to the millions of people connected to education. This creates the brand.

All of these people have contributed something to the pictures in the audience's mind relating to education (and to a particular school system too). The snippets of information people see or hear about education begin to mesh together, producing a larger mental image of that topic. The more influence educators and schools have in shaping that image, the more control we have over the end perception.

Protecting the brand also becomes part of not only the public relations professional's job, but it is also everyone else's job. It takes only one incident for people to misunderstand what schools do on a daily basis. We can control the perception up to a point, but in some instances, we have to play defense when something goes wrong. Playing defense doesn't always mean swatting at questions thrown at the school from reporters, stakeholders, or upset parents; it means that educators know how to protect the rationale for why a decision was made or why an incident happened and then be able to decipher the best way to admit a mistake or explain why a decision was made.

The brand can be tarnished just as easily as the brand can be built. When public relations professionals approach the job of branding as a way of building the culture from the inside out, it's easier to rely on people to build the brand. It's also easier to trust people to make the right decisions and take the best care of students when they understand how important they are in creating or diminishing the brand.

How tightly the brand is controlled will be a personal preference for public relations professionals, but letting other educators in on the responsibility will provide benefits beyond the professional's control. Train principals, teachers, and students to understand their role in building the capacity of the brand. Let them help.

After all is said and done, when the people connected to school can continually praise and appreciate the work being done there, have opportunities to see what happens there, and can feel strong positive emotions about what happens there, the brand has been established.

THE PRINCIPAL

The media has a difficult job. It must find the stories that will draw people's interest and ire. Often the stories that are reported involve glamorization or sensations to peak interest. The breaking news or the pieces that are provocative or involve celebrities usually are the headlines that are memorable. And in a matter of hours, the old news is out and new updated stories are taking its place. But very few of these stories involve all the wonderful elements of schools. Schools have so much to celebrate. Yet we rarely take the time to celebrate and share our stories with the outside audience.

This mentality needs to change. Some of the most iconic symbols speak to a company's brand: the golden arches, the swoosh, an apple with a bite taken out of it, a siren wearing a crown with long, flowing hair. Schools must be the storytellers, the chief information officers, the branding agents. Schools need to share the stories they want to share with the community.

Unfortunately, the reality is that if schools do not tell their own stories, someone else is going to do so on their behalf. Schools should be the ones telling the stories, celebrating the learning, and connecting with the families and community. When it comes to a school's brand, there are several elements that need to be incorporated: a school's purpose and mission, school traditions, and learning celebrations.

When was the last time you heard a school talk about its purpose and mission? Most people know that a school's purpose and mission is to promote and increase student learning. However true that is, that is just one purpose of schools. When thinking about branding for school, start with the question *what do we want our school to be known for?* and that will help begin the conversation.

This conversation can involve stakeholders. If this question were posed to parents and families, what would they say? If this question were posed to staff members, what would they say? If this question were posed to students, what would they say? Do all the answers align or does each stakeholder group have different opinions as to what the school should be known for? If all the answers are aligned, you know your brand.

If your answers are not aligned, bring the stakeholders together to help show them what you want the brand to be. To help align the beliefs of the varying stakeholder groups, use a quality tool such as a SWOT (strengths, weaknesses, opportunities, and threats) analysis to help facilitate the discussion. Figure 8.9 is an example of a SWOT analysis form to use in facilitating the discussion.

	Helpful to achieving the objective	Harmful to achieving the objective
Internal Origin (attributes of the school)	Strengths	Weaknesses
External Origin (attributes of the environment)	Opportunities	Threats

Figure 8.9. SWOT Analysis

Using a SWOT analysis will allow for discussions that help clarify the purpose and the brand of a school. Examining the strengths, weaknesses, and opportunities for improvements and the potential threats will help each stakeholder group work collaboratively to identify a brand for the school.

Once the brand has been developed and consensus has been reached on the question *what do we want our school to be known for,* now it is time to tell the story. Promote this brand through social media, word of mouth, on the school marquee, and in printed newsletters. Share this brand. Own this brand. Be proud of this brand. Make this brand represent all the hard work and effort into making the school what it is today and what it needs to be in the future.

Have main talking points relating to your brand. Enlist the help of the district public relations director to come visit with the staff to share effective ways to communicate the message.

Every school has its traditions that make it unique, special, and connected with itself and the local community. Perhaps it is the staff versus students kickball game, or the Veteran's Day fireside chats, or the career share days with moms and dads, or the schoolwide field day, or the sending off of the seniors by walking through the halls with the drum line, or the junior year community service projects, or the mom and son dance, or the seniors of the year ceremony.

What traditions make up a school? How are these traditions promoted? How do schools continue these time-honored traditions? Sharing these stories and traditions works to enhance the brand. Let the audience hear these stories so everyone can experience schools and their spirit.

Maybe most importantly, a school's brand is the vehicle through which it shares the learning occurring each day. Educators are fortunate enough to see what happens in a classroom on a daily basis. Unfortunately, families and community members do not have the same privilege.

A school's brand exists to tell the stories that do not make the television or newspaper headlines. Think of the student who made tremendous growth in her reading abilities this year. How does a school tell her story? Think of the student who applied his understanding of bar graphs and his knowledge of football to demonstrate a running back's yards per season over time. How does a school tell his story? Think of the student who is a peer tutor to another student and spends part of recess helping this younger student learn to add and subtract. How does a school tell their story? Think of the student who came up with the idea to have a school store selling items with the school mascot on them. How does a school tell his story? Think of the teacher who organized a flashlight drive for the homeless in his hometown to have light in the nighttime. How does a school tell his story?

The reality is that if these stories are not told, the larger audience will never know. These are the stories we want to share. These are the stories schools need to share. These are the stories that make schools have an image and a brand. If these stories are not told by the school, they will not be told. Schools need to be marketing and branding aficionados that share their purpose and mission, their traditions, and their examples of learning occurring in schools.

When the focus is on the positive stories and traditions of a school and its brand, all the leaders in a school—students, staff, and families—can be proud of the school and what its community has to offer. Sharing these positive stories is a way to promote the good happening in schools.

These stories can be told in a variety of ways. And through the use of technology and social media tools, these stories can be told by students, families, and staff members. These stories can be shared on the school's website; through the school's blog; through the school's Twitter, Facebook, or Instagram accounts; and through word of mouth.

Share these stories via YouTube. Have students broadcast their learning and their and the school's message to families and the community. Students are often the best storytellers since they experience the culture firsthand. Let their student voices be heard.

The method of delivery is not as important as making sure the message and story are shared. Shout it from the rooftops for all to hear.

SUMMARY

Go shout it from the rooftops. Share what you want the audience to know about your message. The brand becomes our story. The images become our story. The people become our story. The words become our story. Harness the images, people, and words. Make the mission be about sharing the brand with students, parents, teachers, and the community. It is all connected. And it's everyone's responsibility.

Build a brand that future generations will look back on and smile, knowing that we built a system of schools that propelled our futures further than anyone ever thought possible. Make the image ingrained in future minds, one that evokes intelligence, academia, childhood, and strong positive emotions. Education has a brand. It's up to all educators to make it continually better.

NINE

The Reader's Turn

The public relations professional and the principal think about the same things, just sometimes not at the same time. Learning and growing together provides all the people working within school districts the opportunity to be better. The art of learning from each other is more accessible today than ever before. Schools have to be able to harness the expertise of individual positions and make everyone understand his or her role in both public relations and in teaching and learning.

How educators portray their sense of obligation to the profession shows in their actions and words. As a reader of this book, you are interested in combining the expertise of different professions within a school system. You understand an obligation to portray yourself in a manner worthy of the pedestal educators should stand upon.

It is all educators' responsibilities to go into their schools and be the people our students need them to be. In turn, it then becomes an educator's responsibility to be better, learn more deeply, listen carefully, and collaborate effectively.

Explore ways that you can learn about a colleague's job. Think of yourself as a public relations spokesperson, a teacher, a principal, a superintendent, a coach, a student, and a parent. Each of these roles contributes to a school community. Dabble in another person's path, and then walk on your own. As educators, we like to learn. Be selfish in learning about the things you want to learn about. And learn about lots of different areas of education.

Public relations professionals are strategic partners within school districts. This means that public relations professionals hold the responsibility to think about all different kinds of ramifications of communication, teaching and learning, social media, events, community, and branding.

Be the person in school districts who thinks three steps ahead of a decision. Think into the future when thinking about what's best for kids.

Principals are also strategic partners within school districts. Principals are the core leaders of schools. They think about taking care of students, teachers, and their neighborhoods. They give. They think about the future and they want what's best for kids as well. Along with public relations professionals and all other educators, principals fight for the future of our schools.

You don't need a gimmick to sell education. Our product (education) is easily sellable as long as it comes from a place of high achievement, integrity, and authenticity. Our students shine as examples of a quality product. Be cognizant of your role as an educator in showcasing our students and the work we all do in schools. Find ways to make your story about students and schools stick, meaning find ways to make the passion you have for schools catch on. Make others understand the magic you experience in your schools.

What we as educators feel and experience as we work with all kinds of people in our communities is the gusto that keeps our society connected. The richness of our connections to kids and families solidifies what we all want for the betterment of our communities. We all want to be bound to a better place. Education provides the opportunity to tie ourselves to that notion.

Go out and get to work. Be part of the educators creating stories. Have a positive impact on learning. It's your turn.

Afterword

In our era of competition where parents choose their schools, the advice of Kelly and Matt Wachel gives us strategic advice on how we need to focus our communication and engagement efforts. They understand the critical importance of providing substance to our messages that communicate just what all great schools and systems are about—learning, teaching, and achievement.

Teaming up for this effort is a great collaboration, as it gives firsthand, real-world approaches by two experienced professionals. Kelly, a veteran school communicator, knows what works with parents and the greater community when talking about public relations strategies and tactics dealing with today's perceptions of public education. Matt, a principal and education leader, realistically sees this mission of communication and engagement from the inside out. His working with teachers, students, and parents for many years gives us the insight to focus on what's really important in today's schools.

In addition, the Wachels also help to define what achievement really means. They note achievement needs to first talk about the progress we are making with all our children—not just standardized test scores. When all children come to us, we need to show parents and others just how much progress their children have made and continue to make. Parents appreciate that type of communication a great deal more than a score on a state or national test. By connecting with parents about their children, we all become partners in the *achievement process* that *we call school*. By demonstrating progress at all levels, you will quickly build your brand and a positive reputation for your teachers, staff, and all your schools.

Additional points to use from this great resource follow:

- Schools do a multitude of tasks, but overall, each school has to show what it is doing around learning. We also need to ask the question, "How are we preparing our students to be successful for their future?"

Amen to that! That is exactly what a school needs to communicate. Keeping the focus on learning shows you care about each child and reaps the results to build community consensus that your school is a great school. And that is a great place to be in our era of parental choice.

- All those in education are spokespeople for the schools in which they work.

Our work indicates that teachers and other school employees are seen as the most credible spokespeople when it comes to their schools. Makes sense to me. If you really want to know about a restaurant or an auto repair shop, you ask questions of the people who work there. We need to continue to work with our staff members at all levels to engage them in making their schools a much better place to work and learn. Once they are engaged in and believe in what they do every day, they will begin telling more people about it.

Another key point under this heading is that it really is everyone's job to communicate about his or her schools. Often, we see staff members pointing to the communication pro in their district as the communicator and note that communication is not part of their job description. All employees have the responsibility to communicate, and districts need to provide assistance in making that happen. Help teachers and others provide insight to parents on how their children are learning and making progress.

- Makerspaces provide a space for students to wonder and invite them to research on some of their wonderings.

Perceptions of what is going on in schools today are often filled with wide gaps from reality. When parents and others can see how children are working together on interesting projects, they soon begin to see the need for collaboration, critical thinking, communication, and creativity. Getting folks to see today's schools in action is a great myth and perception buster when communicating about today's schools.

- The question is not are you using social media? The question is how are you using social media?

A second amen to this one! Schools and school districts are quickly jumping into the social media arena, and they do need to be there for many good reasons. Many of your school audiences are there, so you need to be there too. But the "how" you are using it and "why" you are using it may need some scrutiny. Strategic social media offerings will help others understand the progress and achievement elements mentioned throughout this book. Just doing social media may be fun and cool, and that can be fine as long as it is occasional and not the bulk of your efforts. Find ways to demonstrate progress and achievement though "free" social media platforms with the many examples listed throughout the book.

If you are serious about making a communication impact for your schools, follow the Wachels' advice and insight and you will be on your way to planning a path to communication success. Just remember that reading the book is one thing, but making a plan and taking action is the only way you will begin making a difference through your substantive communication efforts. And most importantly, be proactive in your communication work—otherwise you will always be catching up to what others are saying about your schools. I often say, "You need to be out front so you will not be left behind."

Thanks to the Wachels for this contribution to the body of knowledge in our school communication profession.

Rich Bagin, APR

National School Public Relations Association (NSPRA) Executive Director